Praise for *Leading with Head and Heart*

"Research tells us that school administrators set the climate and quality instruction and that they are a major factor in determining whether leave or stay in high-needs schools. Leadership can be quite rewarding. Yet, many who ascend to leadership also agree that it is easy to focus on impersonal tasks and lose sight of what brought them to education in the first place—the desire to help others and shape the future. That's where *Leading with Head and Heart* comes in. Through thought-provoking vignettes, relevant and relatable experiences, and practical approaches this book will energize both aspiring and veteran school leaders. They will be motivated to connect or reconnect with their passion and inspire students, staff, and their communities to thrive."

—Lisa Corbin, educational consultant

"As a longtime educator and director of leadership development, I found Anthony Colannino's book, *Leading with Head and Heart*, to be a dynamic and engaging guide for what leaders need in order to move their school communities forward during this turbulent and fast-paced time. This book will help aspiring and current leaders pay attention to often overlooked factors such as courage, vulnerability, and empathy, in addition to effective strategies, in order to maximize their influence and impact."

—John D'Auria, EdD director, Educational
Leadership Concentration, William James College

"Anthony Colannino envisions an education system in which our work to improve learning and to care for and inspire those we serve are interdependent aims. This shift in educational philosophy is not new. But the timing of Anthony's call to action is. There has never been a more important time to read this book and to answer this call."

—Dr. Amy Fast, principal, McMinnville High School

"In a world where we are in the midst of historic times, many have asked themselves, both in moments of quiet reflection and with others, what must be done to advance humankind. In this book, Anthony speaks not only to the minds of educators but just as equally to their hearts. He shows us the path to understanding the environments that not only constitute our current reality but also can be the precursors for future innovation and impact. Connect with and go deeper in this book. Remember that one, just one, idea can change your life forever in a phenomenal way. I challenge you to find that one idea in this book. Your future starts today."

—Vernon Wright, entrepreneur; speaker; NLP Life Coach; consultant;
leader; influencer; founder, ZeroApologyZone.com

Leading
with Head
and Heart

A Practical Guide to Elevating the School
of Today—and Tomorrow

Anthony Colannino

International Center for
Leadership in Education.

International Center for Leadership in Education, Inc.
1587 Route 146
Rexford, New York 12148
www.LeaderEd.com
info@LeaderEd.com

ISBN: 978-0-358-56854-4

International Center For Leadership In Education
is a division of Houghton Mifflin Harcourt.

Printed in the United States of America.

1 2 3 4 5 6 7 8 9 10 0304 30 29 28 27 26 25 24 23 22 21

4500825599 ABCD

Contents

For my greatest Uncle Bob and Aunt Blanca.
You filled my head and heart with love, joy, and whimsy.

Acknowledgments

I am passionate about writing and education—teaching, leading, and learning. Combining these two passions in book-length form has been exciting and exhausting, and I've needed to be tethered or buoyed, depending on the moment. Consequently, although this book has my name on the cover, it took a village to get it in your hands.

In book creation and development, I had three writing professionals in my corner to whom I offer my sincere thanks. Kate Gagnon, director of professional publications at Houghton Mifflin Harcourt, has been discussing this book with me for more than two years. These discussions took many forms, from exploratory—What do you want to write about?—to the nitty-gritty of form, language, and theme. She has been a foundation for what finally appears on the pages that follow. Editor Julie Kendrick's patience, persistence, and care made a huge difference in helping me move beyond initial ideas in rough outline form to polished, focused chapters. Her involvement ranged from carefully nudging me along to expertly cutting extraneous or repetitive text. Julie did all that with organization, humor, and precision. Jeff Leeson, editorial director of Benson Collister, provided a 35,000-foot view for clarity and fueled my sense of purpose by asking all the right questions and offering targeted suggestions. These included his thoughts on book design, the table of contents, and chapter formation; there was really nothing outside Jeff's purview or direction.

For all those in the book production and publishing world I will never meet and who worked on *Leading with Head and Heart*, I thank you, including designers, editors, production staff, and marketing. I am humbled by the many professionals whose commitment, professionalism, and skill made this book possible.

There are leaders you will meet throughout *Leading with Head and Heart*, and all were generous with their time and experiences. I owe these leaders a deep debt of gratitude for allowing me to fold their stories into mine: in order of appearance, Dr. Kyle Heath, superintendent of Cleburne, Texas, Independent School District (ISD); Lisa Votaw, principal of Aiken High School in Cincinnati, Ohio; Dr. Adrian Mims, founder of The Calculus Project; Toney Jackson, fourth-grade teacher from Nellie K. Parker School in Hackensack, New Jersey; Kent Brewer, principal of Linton-Stockton Elementary School in Indiana; Jeff Dees, principal of Upham Elementary in Wellesley, Massachusetts; Annette Addair, principal of Galveston Elementary School in Chandler, Arizona; Terry Roller, chief administrative officer for the Alabama State Department of Education; Dr. Robert Bowman, superintendent of Naches Valley School District in Naches, Washington; Dr. James Hickey, headmaster of Austin Preparatory School in Reading, Massachusetts; Antonio Acuña, principal of Del Valle High School in El Paso, Texas; and Kathy Baumgardner, principal of Asbury Park High School in Asbury, New Jersey. Each leader also read his or her chapter for accuracy.

Although several friends and colleagues read some of my manuscript, my cousin, Mary Murphy, colleague, Dr. Lisa Corbin, and Twitter friend, Taylor Armstrong, read it from start to finish, providing invaluable edits and feedback.

My experiences of teaching and leadership did not happen in isolation. Students, teachers, support staff, parents, caregivers, colleagues, and mentors all have affected me in meaningful ways. Please know every time I have led, presented, coached, and written, I have brought all of you to everything I do. You have made me better by listening, participating, following, questioning, challenging, and willingly building something better together with me.

A few people I must mention include Jim Walsh, a mentor to so many leaders, and John D'Auria, who always makes me better in his presence. They are the kind of leaders I still aspire to become. Sue Delahunt, school adjustment counselor at MacArthur Elementary, revealed a more therapeutic approach to helping children struggling socially and emotionally at school. Her guidance and countenance elevated my leadership with children and adults alike. Sharon Grossman, school psychologist at Fiske Elementary, was instrumental in all aspects of school life, from testing and servicing the needs of our most vulnerable children to improving school culture. She continues to be a strong moral compass for doing what's right. Finally, former literacy specialist at MacArthur, Nancy Coppolino, held passions for reading, the students she taught, the teachers she coached, and the city of Waltham. She inspired me to do more and be better. I always felt as if anything was possible in Nancy's presence, and there are never enough of these types of colleagues in the world. I was lucky to work with her and will never forget her.

At home during a pandemic, writing a book wasn't such a solitary experience with my wife, Kara, and my two children, Joseph and Stella, working and learning at home for part or most of this writing. This is not to say it made the work easier or harder, just different. Because my attention can be variable and changeable, "my office" was in the common area where TV watching, cooking, eating, and passing by occurred often. As a result, it was impossible for me to ignore my family or for them to ignore me. Maybe in this disruptive year of 2020, this was a good thing. Still Kara, Joseph, Stella, as well as our dog, Finley, had to put up with long instances without engagement from me at all hours when I felt inspired or compelled to write. In all, Finley was the most disagreeable and persistent in demanding my attention for walks, food, water, and play. Without my family, this book was neither possible nor important, because they inspire me to be a better person while tolerating my shortcomings.

About the Author

Anthony Colannino has taught, led, and consulted in schools for more than twenty years, following a brief career in journalism. He's witnessed firsthand the power of a kind word at the right time, the positive response when dignity is offered, and the difference educators can make in the lives of children. He is buoyed by the hope an effective education holds for all our students, which in turn improves schools, districts, communities, countries, and the world.

When not writing, he loves a great short story, skiing, and watching thoroughbred horses run in circles. He lives with his wife, Kara; two children, Joseph and Stella; and their dog, Finley, just north of Boston.

Connect with Anthony online and learn more about his mission, vision, and passion here:
www.leadingandteachingforgrowth.com

About the International Center for Leadership in Education

The International Center for Leadership in Education (ICLE), a division of Houghton Mifflin Harcourt, challenges, inspires, and equips leaders and teachers to prepare their students for lifelong success. At the heart of all we do is the proven philosophy that the entire system must be aligned around instructional excellence—rooted in rigor, relevance, and relationships—to ensure every student is prepared for a successful future.

Founded in 1991 by Dr. Bill Daggett, ICLE, through its team of thought leaders and consultants, partners with schools and districts to implement innovative practices to scale through professional learning opportunities guided by the cornerstones of our work: the Daggett System for Effective Instruction® and the Rigor/Relevance Framework®. Additionally, ICLE shares successful practices that have a positive impact on student learning through keynote presentations, the Model Schools Conference, and a rich collection of publications. Learn more at LeaderEd.com.

Introduction
A Leader's Head and Heart

We stand at a moment in history when sorting out the means for daily delivery of teaching and learning and building structures for future innovations of improved pedagogy, policy, and technology are equally important. How school leaders of all kinds deliver on the needs of today and tomorrow will define our schools for the next fifty years. Dealing with the stress of the most pressing concerns of the day, while simultaneously looking ten years into a better future, presents multifaceted challenges for all school leaders.

My goal in writing *Leading with Head and Heart* is to offer help to these leaders. If there ever was a time to step back, take a collective breath, and reconsider education leadership, it is now. Schools must respond to today's—and tomorrow's—challenges with cultures of inclusion and growth. Leaders everywhere struggle to not only maintain a standard of learning but also to somehow create new pathways for equitable opportunity and seize on technological advances that can improve learning. How leadership delivers on these imperatives, now and later, matters. But although we know new priorities will keep arising that require shifts in focus, what remains constant will be a framework of leading that can respond effectively, regardless of where changes must be made.

When leaders have too many urgent decisions in front of them, it's exceedingly difficult to see the horizon of growth and innovation in the distance. A day—or mere hours—just ahead of a crisis is no place to create strategic plans for the future. School systems everywhere are overwhelmed by problems that they lack the methodology or mindsets to respond to effectively. This leaves leaders feeling helpless and teachers feeling uncertain. It's impossible to plan for a pandemic, tornado, or widespread reckoning with social injustice. What is possible is to build leadership skills that originate in a leader's head and heart. Once this happens, leaders can develop school, department, and classroom cultures that drive toward greater, more equitable, educational gains.

The Difference between Head and Heart

Too often, we delineate between our heads and hearts—the logic and emotion of living—as if they're separate identities pulling in opposite directions away from an individual perspective. *Leading with Head and Heart* examines how together your head and heart can inform your leadership. This may reaffirm your leadership style or challenge your thinking in a way you find disruptive. Both phases of thinking about yourself and how you lead have the potential to enlighten your intention and direction. As Nelson Mandela said, "A good head and a good heart are always a formidable combination."

Depending on your position on the leadership spectrum—from neophyte to seasoned veteran—you've likely been exposed to a multitude of leadership research, approaches, and styles. You probably have defined yourself first and foremost as a certain kind of leader, such as instructional, therapeutic, transformative, servant, or data-driven. Even if you haven't consciously chosen a style, your words, beliefs, behaviors, and stories have already defined your style to your followers.

Leading with Head and Heart can inform any of these approaches and even cause you to reflect more deeply and intentionally on your leadership style. There's a complexity to achieving a balance of head and heart, especially if this is a new way of thinking for you. But fear not; acknowledgment of the difficulty is a first step toward achieving it.

Fortunately, there is also a simplicity in developing a unified approach with your head informing your heart—or vice versa—when you fully consider the ramifications of each tactic. Responding with your head can center your focus on logical outcomes that can become automatic over time: A student or teacher acts out in a certain way and a logical consequence occurs, a school improvement plan is formed and accepted by a school board, or a budget shortfall is discovered that needs remedying through a tax levy.

When you act with your heart, you consider the emotions of the participants in the moment and how they may evolve over time. A student or teacher acts out in a certain way, and you ask curious, empathetic questions to find the appropriate response. Or a school improvement plan's formation is fraught with disagreement—how do you appeal to all stakeholders in order to resolve it? Or when a budget shortfall emerges and several remedies are presented, how will school values be represented in making financial decisions? These actions take shape in the heart.

In these examples, you can see how your head and heart are more closely aligned than you may have thought. Identifying head and heart considerations with yourself and your staff members, students, families, district, and community will better inform your leadership.

Leading is not easy, but we complicate matters when what we really should be doing is asking simple questions, such as "Is this really what's best for our students, staff members, or families?" Beyond determining what's best, we must invest ourselves fully in working through the obstacles that often present themselves with a methodology to do so. *Leading with Head and Heart* will provide a jumping-off point and a confirmation of directions taken that can become routines of excellence.

Who This Book Is For

Leaders are found everywhere in schools, from those with titles and degrees to those who have been anointed by their colleagues as informal experts on matters of culture or curriculum. *Leading with Head and Heart* has been written with all forms of leaders in mind. The formal leaders within schools, central office administration, department heads, and curriculum coordinators have all been considered in the stories and ideas presented within the book. In addition, those in quasi-administrative roles will find solace in the pages that follow. This includes instructional coaches, support staff members for defined student populations (such as special education and multilingual learners), and those charged with delivering instruction, modeling, or coaching on districtwide initiatives without supervisory powers to enforce them.

Teachers, the largest group to work in schools, hold distinct leadership experiences not only within their grade levels and content teams but also in how they infuse their interest and enthusiasm for learning in all that they do, which can and does go unnoticed. In the pages that follow, narratives and experiences are provided to recognize leadership that often starts in the classroom and should be tapped for improvement throughout a school or district.

Support staff members of all kinds—from those maintaining the grounds, tending to sick students, and ensuring mental health needs—will see themselves in head and heart stories as well.

Finding meaning and inspiration through leadership is foundational throughout this book. This is often reflected in the experiences of school leaders across the country, as well as my own experiences. Topics in the book that are tied directly to our emotions—such as love, empathy, dignity, and vulnerability—all speak to our hearts and how we lead through our feelings. But chapters also include the more discrete skills that we associate with our heads, including sections devoted to culture, equity (twice), and clarity in communication. In the culminating chapter of the book, courage is examined through the prism of a cadre of leaders who have successfully merged head and heart in their leadership practice.

Leading with Head and Heart pulls back the curtain on leadership, exposing the quiet triumphs and anxious moments all leaders face. Here are some examples of leaders you will meet throughout the book:

- A state administrator in the Deep South who recalls his fear of failure and the coach's words that helped guide him to a life of service.
- A small-town elementary school principal in middle America who knew he had to incorporate love into his leadership style and began by announcing to his students and staff members every day, "If no one has told you they love you today, know that I love you."
- A big-city high school principal in the Southwest who knows all of his 2,100 students on a first-name basis, sees just about all of them graduate on time, and sets high standards through constantly communicating clearly with his faculty members and students.
- A teacher and dean who refused to believe Black students couldn't learn advanced placement math and started his own grassroots leadership program, The Calculus Project, to prove it.

Through their eyes, and mine, you will find an inspiring level of idealism, but it's an idealism that is always grounded with plenty of pragmatic takeaways. In fact, you'll find five takeaways, called "Reflections on How Life Should Be," at the end of each chapter. Other special features that you'll find throughout the book include thoughtful vignettes called "Mindset Moments" and action items called "Today and Tomorrow."

What Happens Next

We currently stand at an educational crossroads, with multiple pathways leading to uncertain futures. Yes, it creates feelings of uncertainty, but it can also be exciting for leaders who can seize the moment and are willing to grow. In responding to the coronavirus pandemic, schools saw the possibilities with designing and implementing learning anywhere and at any time. If leaders can apply themselves to solving today's problems with curricula, pedagogy, and planning, they can also use the same formula to build robust response systems for future challenges.

Creating the best circumstances for learning and growth emanates from how leaders use their heads in concert with their hearts. Considering avenues of thought and feeling together imbues leaders with the skills needed to create and build better systems of learning. Because schools are in the "people-making business," using a humanistic approach seems like common sense. Depending on your role as a leader, your strategies and actions will determine whether children thrive across departments, content areas, schools, and systems. *Leading with Head and Heart* presents an opportunity for you to cultivate and grow your personal leadership skills in a way that elevates these children, as well as honors the potential of every person under your care.

Culture Curation

When I first began my leadership journey, I was lucky enough to meet Jim Walsh, a professor who became a mentor and a confidant. He served for thirteen years as superintendent of the Brookline, Massachusetts, schools, and he was so beloved by all stakeholders there that the district named the school committee room in his honor. This is no small testament, because school committees and superintendents are often mostly at odds over budgets, policy, pedagogy, and more. But there was something welcoming about Jim that enabled people to set aside their differences. He had a genuine interest in anyone who was sitting across from him, even during disagreements.

Jim was a heavy-set guy, and his tie and shirt would bend to the arc of his belly. He listened intently and was forever ready with wise words about leading, learning, and just being a better person. I often shared my frustrations and fascinations with Jim, including a time when I was teaching fifth grade in Cambridge, Massachusetts. I was not getting along with my principal, and I called Jim to unload a long list of perceived transgressions on poor me. He heard me out and then gave me advice I have never forgotten. "Anthony, do you really want to contribute to this person's demise?"

I remember stopping in my tracks, jaw hanging open, with nothing to say. This wasn't just because Jim was right, but because, in that moment, he was able to transform my frustration into reflection. I told him, "No, Jim, I don't want to contribute to anyone else's demise." Seeming to read my mind, Jim provided further perspective on the difficulty of leading, noting that my principal had just returned from a maternity leave after the birth of her first child, and couldn't I imagine how challenging it was to lead and raise a child? I wondered why I couldn't have considered this principal's personal situation before becoming so angry at her. It wasn't the first or the last time Jim made me reflect, reaffirm, change, or challenge my thinking. It's my hope that I can provide the same role for you as we travel this leadership journey. We'll be considering how our heads and hearts provide the foundation to become leaders, perhaps eventually becoming more like Jim, who showed others the way.

Culture was of paramount importance to Jim, which is evident by this truism he taught me: "There are three things you have to do when you become a leader: First, learn the culture. Second, honor the culture. Third, when it's necessary, change the culture." Jim died more than ten years ago, but his words still roll through my head, lighting a path for my own personal development. And isn't eternity the seeds we plant in others when we support them, showing them what's possible, a hope for a not-so-distant future? Jim did this for me, so much so that Jim's name and number still sit in my phone's contact list. It's a reminder of his words, presence, and wisdom I can't do without.

Creating a Culture Together

Learning school cultures began my journey into considering how I must also curate them. This meant gathering strengths that weren't always evident, exposing weaknesses and their outcomes, understanding limited and important changes that could be made, and creating consensus among all stakeholders. Before unveiling their plans and their brilliance, leaders willing to curate from those they lead, or will lead, take the following actions first:

- Inventory the current culture and conditions of the people and processes that predate the leader.
- Provide informal and formal ways to receive feedback on personal perspectives from all stakeholders on what it's like to work and live in this environment.
- Report back on findings and common themes revealed from actively listening to comments, concerns, suggestions, and ideas from stakeholders.
- Share the why, how, and what will be held sacred, develop new avenues of support, and infuse an energy and enthusiasm into defining what it means to be part of this community.
- Create or focus on values that are present or need to be present.

Jim knew that culture superseded strategy. Ultimately—he would tell me—a poorly defined culture will stop any attempts at growth right in its tracks. If leadership fails to understand, define, and harness the power of culture curation in addressing whatever shifts in pedagogy, funding, or research inevitably arise during any leader's tenure, then it will become impossible to address them adequately. A culture of resistance will pervade any meaningful changes if culture isn't curated first.

I've learned to view culture as Jim did. It can be nebulous when left undefined, and that can lead to ineffective schools or to a culture void that ultimately will be filled with whatever others choose. From those with good intentions to those with a chip on their shoulder, leaving culture to be loosely curated outside a leader's intentions is culture by default, and it is ultimately directionless.

Defining Culture Where You Lead

Culture, weak or strong, will pervade everything you and your schools do, and I do mean *everything*. The only way to be successful in curating a culture of mission, vision, and inclusion is to first learn the culture of the classroom, school, or district you've been charged with leading.

At its core, culture is a feeling you get when you walk into a room, school, or conference room. Are there people engaged with each other personally and professionally, showing care and compassion as well as vision and mission? Is there joy and passion in the triumph and the challenge? What does it mean to live and learn in this class, this school, this district?

Actually, asking lots and lots of questions in the hallways, teachers' rooms, custodial offices, classrooms, and conference rooms will provide a gauge for you to first understand the current culture before making any drastic changes. As someone who has been a brand-new leader in a brand-new place many times, I urge you to be careful, intentional, and patient when choosing where and how to place your first leadership stake in the ground because everything else flows from those very first decisions.

Making a positive impact should be the primary objective of your career and your leadership journey. What I mean by *impact* is the ability to play a role in curating a culture that effectively informs, motivates, and, above all, inspires children and adults to learn and grow so they can become their very best selves. When we pour our energies and enthusiasm into helping others grow, we ultimately contribute to the betterment of not only our school's culture but also the communities just beyond the schoolroom doors.

Culture is the sum of beliefs, mindsets, behaviors, and narratives under which a classroom, school, or district exists (see Figure 1.1). First comes

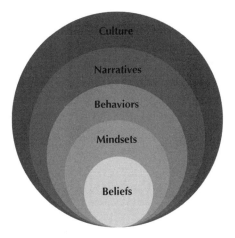

FIGURE 1.1   How a Culture Grows

belief. For a culture to grow and succeed, its foundational belief must be that every student and every adult within a school can learn.

Beliefs, for better or worse, are developed and embedded in our consciousness through direct experiences and also from being passed down by the people who preceded us into adulthood, teaching, and leading. Beliefs can enlighten or feed ignorance—a simpler version of which is not yet knowing and a more entrenched version is when someone is determined to *not* learn but to hold steadfast to prejudicial, hurtful, or even hateful beliefs. That type of ignorance can be passed down and reinforced through personal connections to family and friends, as well as through media of all kinds, including books, social media, movies, and television.

Beliefs can change, but it takes tremendous effort to help those you lead "unlearn" beliefs that are detrimental and wrongheaded or ones that negatively affect the growth potential for all you serve. The singular belief you must have, hold, and cherish is that everyone under your guidance can and does learn, either in response to or in spite of your efforts.

Considering Mindsets

Mindsets are built from beliefs and from experiences with learning. The mindsets that evolve—fixed, mixed, or growth—depend on time, situation, presentation, and understanding.[1] Mindsets drive the collective behaviors that can shape culture.

When you have a growth mindset, you understand that you *can* learn, even when you struggle, that mistakes are part of the challenge of learning, and that when you fail, it is not the end of learning but the beginning. Rising from failure requires self-determination to change or the humility to request the need for a new direction in strategy, feedback, coaching, or skills to overcome the obstacles in your way.

When you are in a fixed mindset, you simply accept failure as an endgame, try to avoid any subject or situation that will expose your weakness, and/or give up on experiences because you weren't perfect when you started. Fixed mindsets foster avoidance and self-preservation that allow us to quit because we feel less than those whom we perceive are meeting success without much effort. A mixed mindset is more about straddling the line between growth and fixed mindsets. It's an uncertainty, open to either a growth or fixed result.

Mindset Moment

A cherished mentor, John D'Auria, respectfully reminded me of the importance of a growth mindset when I was venting frustration with a staff member. Here's how it went:

John: When was the last time you met with this teacher?

Me: I've been avoiding her. I don't even walk down the hallway where her classroom is located.

John: What do you think this teacher takes away from this interaction?

Me: Doesn't feel good about it and is probably worried.

John: What do you think the rest of the staff members take away from watching you avoid this teacher?

[Feeling instantly awful and small] Me: They see that if I disagree or don't like something they're doing, I'll avoid them and abandon them.

[Significant pause] John: You know what you have to do.

I moved from my fixed mindset right then and set out to make amends, prioritize time to talk with the teacher, ask questions of concern, listen intently for understanding, and offer help or support.

The mindsets of those you lead are never as important as the mindset you hold about them. A leader's mindset matters most, not because you're the leader but because your understanding and estimation of your followers will influence their behavior and actions. We all travel the mindset continuum, even those of us with the best intentions, and if we can't recognize it in ourselves, we better have our ears open to all stakeholders, from our youngest students to our most veteran staff members, to be aware of when we've gotten trapped in a fixed mindset and are in danger of derailing all the culture curation work we've done.

Curating, Not Creating

Curation is likely a new way of thinking about culture. Many leaders think of culture as something they must create, but this puts far too much emphasis on a leader. Curation is more about creating culture together—what's in the leader's head and heart is only a starting point to hear, see, and feel what's in everybody else's head and heart—and to understand how it can be tapped for greater access to a new, collective strength. Curation is a collective, not an individual, pursuit.

Consider the concept of fairness, which is significant for teachers, because in many narratives they are treated unfairly—whether it's being burdened with too many students, a lack of resources, new curricula without professional support, or just having a quiet place and a time to eat during the day. Teachers are acutely aware of fairness, and they will notice and point out inequities, especially if there have been past indiscretions or actions from their leaders. Children will point this out in real time as well, but adults also can hold and harbor past hurts, then apply them to the present. I doubt there is a school anywhere in which someone, sometime, doesn't feel the sting of unfair treatment.

Dismissing unfairness as childish or unprofessional because it is curated outside a leader's presence or before a leader's experience would be a mistake. Instead, allow teachers to freely express frustrations in the moment or about those from the past that can negatively affect culture. Curation takes the ability to hear and acknowledge unpleasant circumstances before correcting course.

The Curse of the Successful School

Arriving in a school of success can be fraught with challenges for leadership because the narrative "If it ain't broke, don't fix it" can take hold. Success does not mean growth, because factors such as standardized test scores, GPAs, and college acceptances can easily be correlated to affluence of community more than a school's or system's well-curated culture. I experienced this in Wellesley, Massachusetts, which is a community with multimillion-dollar homes, exclusive clubs, and financially successful families. Curating a growth-minded culture was a challenge at first, as expressed by one parent who told me, "Anthony, I'm all for my third grader learning from mistakes, but how can I let my high school junior fail now, when we're hoping she gets into an Ivy League college?"

Whether a school is struggling or succeeding, how the leader frames culture curation matters. It matters for teachers who might have felt they were treated unfairly, and it matters for parents who are concerned about their children's futures. Whatever was happening, I simply listened over and over again to the current school narrative. This meant grievances could be aired either privately or publicly, restated or acknowledged, before changes were to be made. Finding out the needs, from surface to deep-seated, are the initial steps to understanding a school culture.

Today and Tomorrow

Today. Gauge current culture by surveying staff members with simple questions about what must be honored in this school, how they would like to grow, and what they love about teaching. Gather common data points and share the themes that emerge.

Tomorrow. Create intentional plans for improvement and share them transparently with staff members and stakeholders based on what you've heard. Start by sharing the most crucial rituals that define your school, department, or district. Gather cohorts of staff members to develop future professional learning or more complex, systemic changes. Identify early adopters who can pilot innovations and provide critical feedback before rolling the changes out to an entire staff.

It takes courage to allow a staff member or a parent to state a complaint, misconception, or criticism at a staff or parent teacher association meeting. It also takes some fortitude for a staff member and parent to share. I always considered it an opportunity for me to learn and grow, because if one person felt it strong enough in their heart to say it aloud, I knew five, ten, or more people were thinking the same thing in their heads, too. In this way, curation is a constant formation of past, present, and future stories about what it means to be part of this community. Curation starts when a leader allows the collective in, warts and all.

Once leaders begin curation through curiously seeking input from all, values begin to emerge, along with narratives about the way the teaching and learning happens. Values, whether well-defined or existing only in the perceptions of stakeholders, are foundational and need to be stated clearly for all to follow.

There's Value in Us

Curation takes time and intentionality, because leaders entering any new environment don't yet have a clear understanding of the existing culture. The first step to curating culture is to understand the people who work in that environment, from the boardroom to classroom. A big part of culture curation is simply getting to know your stakeholders—students, staff members, families, department heads, building leaders, and board members, depending on your role. You want a winning strategy to help understand culture? Learn the name of everyone you work with directly, and then learn the names of everyone else that you can.

Learning names is a culture builder. First, it's respectful to greet people by their name. If you happen to wander into a department, school, or classroom where you don't know the people, simply ask their names and use them. Once you get to know people's names, then you are far more likely to ask your followers, associates, or colleagues something about themselves. When you get to know these people, they'll begin to reveal more details, not only about themselves but also about where they work. You're more likely to find out what's going well, where they need support, or to hear an idea or innovation they've been considering or have already put in place.

Jim Walsh, that bastion of culture curation I mentioned at the beginning of this chapter, not only knew this but also lived it. As superintendent, he made it his business to learn every staff member's name, more than five hundred in all. That's a lot of names, but he took the time to know and learn them, and his staff members responded with devotion and dedication. On his passing, a central office staff member remarked that "he even knew the custodians by name."

I felt so strongly about being on a first-name basis that I did as Jim did. The only promise I made entering a new school as its leader was that I would know every student's name before Thanksgiving break. It was a promise I kept in all four buildings in which I was principal. Those schools ranged in size from 250 to 400 students, so it wasn't an easy task. Knowing everyone by name was all about living the culture and values that I wanted to understand, honor, and support. When I know you by name, I am bound to also know something about you. Whether it's an interest, news about your life, or something that may be bothering you, you're far more likely to let me know when we are connected on a first-name basis.

Strong Cultures, Strong Values

Strong cultures exist when everyone feels as if he or she belongs, has a voice, and is supported. Building a voice in all stakeholders should be the first strategy for growth, a response to challenge, or preparation for innovation. Culture provides the structure to communicate values daily. Whenever I asked stakeholders what I needed to value as I entered the schools I led, I received a host of answers that included what it felt like to work in the school, the rituals I had to honor, and policies and procedures that needed to change. By asking questions of individuals, I was provided a road map for success for all as common elements of past and present culture were revealed. I was able to see what the school needed to do to improve. The "why" of getting there was a large part of my curation.

I've worked in schools where the values were already stated, ones where they needed to be reinforced, and ones where they were nonexistent. Values start with each individual and what that person brings to his or her position and become magnified through a prism of agreed-on values that are followed, especially when the business of learning gets hard.

The Free Book Fiasco

It's inevitable that at some points in your leadership, it will get very hard, so prepare yourself for that eventuality. Sometimes it will be unexpected and surprising how difficulties arise. I felt this surprise on the very first steps of my leadership practicum when I tried to provide free books for teachers.

I was teaching teachers of grades three through five about guided reading instruction. We had just started our thirty-six hours together when I proposed additional books leveled for all readers to fortify classroom libraries. Great idea, right? It seemed that way, until I asked the teachers what books they would buy, and a third- and fourth-grade teacher got into a heated argument about who should teach *The Trumpet of the Swan*, a book they both unwittingly had been teaching for years. Something I thought would be easy and fun quickly disintegrated into something riddled with complications I had not foreseen. Worse, we had no stated value systems to fall back on, and I simply had to rescue the situation by telling both teachers we'd talk about it later.

Values define us, and adhering to them as a team, school, department, or district gives them real power because of the momentum that is built by practicing them in any number of situations. Through planning, assessing, responding, evaluating, and, yes, disciplining, values are revisited and demonstrated for all.

What exists in our heads and hearts is given an external outlet daily by actions or lack of actions that our values demand. If your school or department holds the value of empathy, and you find yourself in a situation in which you aren't showing it, you're falling short. A value that has been defined, modeled, and practiced becomes socially normed into place and practiced through a collective pressure to act on it. This is how a culture is curated—through the gentle or strong pressure that forces us to act on and through it.

Communicating Shared Values

Some schools do a great job of making sure everyone is on board with shared values, which become the cornerstone of their culture. Here's an example: When I arrived as the brand-new principal at Fiske Elementary

School in Wellesley, Massachusetts, the school had already agreed on a set of values that formed an acronym for the school name:

- Fair
- Inclusive
- Safe
- Kind
- Encouraging

We sang about these values at our school-wide, community meetings; chose read-aloud books that demonstrated them; had a main office bulletin board where teachers and students could highlight one another exhibiting those values; and spoke about them when students and adults failed to live up to them. When students broke a value, a scripted discussion ensued:

- Which value did you break?
- How did you break the value?
- What was a result of your action?
- What have or do you need to learn as a result?

In these ways, we modeled and lived our values daily. As a leader, I already had the foundation to build on in curating culture, even before my first actions of leadership at Fiske. I was rewarded for embracing the culture wholeheartedly, because, at my parent interview, a father asked me to recite the school values. Because I had already studied and memorized them, I was able to recite them back to him. Interview score!

Each day there were hundreds, if not thousands, of thoughts, discussions, and actions in accordance with our Fiske values by students, teachers, and caregivers. These values became a natural of part of how the business of learning occurred, because they lived in all the classrooms, offices, playgrounds, and wherever our students and teachers traveled.

Because they were constantly reinforced and normed, the values weren't just mine as a principal. They belonged to everyone. Our beliefs, mindsets, behaviors, and narratives were socially normed to define, follow, and celebrate our values because we had so many outlets for our constant and active observance of them. Children and adults knew the expectations individually and collectively so they breathed life into our values, which simply became a way of being.

It's always heartwarming and humbling to witness values become a guiding light in troubled times. Cleburne Independent School District, an eleven-school district an hour southwest of Dallas, Texas, was fortunate enough to take on its values discussion and definition to start the 2019–2020 school year, just months before the coronavirus pandemic forced school closures in March. School superintendent Dr. Kyle Heath credits his district's effective response to COVID-19 to first determining, and then following, the district's newly adopted core values of excellence, shown in Figure 1.2.

The catchphrase for these values is "Knowing everyone by name, need, and strength." Students are at the top of the chart, defined as a value, which is very much intentional. In fact, whatever Cleburne ISD is doing together, from developing a budget to writing a curriculum, begins with one question: "Is this what's best for students?" In this view, all other values flow from doing what's best for students, and therein lies the district's call to action in any given situation.

Doing what's best for students infuses every Cleburne department. From food services, business, and maintenance to those departments that provide direct support to students—all are focused on the social emotional well-being of children. This common value is shared by all, because the question about doing what's best for students is asked consistently and constantly, holding each department accountable and working beyond fragile egos or incomplete perspectives, and instead gathering the strength behind what is a shared, curated, and collective agency of all.

Cleburne's sharp focus on students has also been buoyed by their second value statement on relationships: to "build a foundation of trust, communication, and collaboration" for all stakeholders. In summer 2019, this started with modeling what this meant for all relationships. District and school leaders held meetings with each other, their staff members, and their students. Dr. Heath made it a practice to take time during leadership meetings for building stronger relationships with everyone around the table. All of his cabinet members were able to see firsthand how he expects all district, school, and classroom relationships to be formed.

"I can't stress enough how our newly adapted core values of excellence guided us through changing instruction on a dime during the pandemic's outbreak," Heath says. "Each adult felt the need to contribute to a common

FIGURE 1.2   Cleburne Independent School District Core Values of Excellence

cause, breathing life into our values and how we defined what made Cleburne ISD successful and special."

Culture curation through a shared value system allows for contributions big and small. Starting with a common goal of defining what it means to be part of a class, department, school, and district, adults and students can build the trusting relationships necessary for meaningful learning, wherever it occurs. Everyone needs an avenue to enter school environments based on strong relationships formed, which leads to greater learning throughout a school or district.

From Compliance to Culture

Culture is derived from a shared set of values expressed in many different ways. No two cultures are the same. It is the stuff of mission statements, but only as a means, not an end. Too many mission statements are artfully written and then collect dust behind picture frames or within bookshelves. All missions need to live and be reaffirmed, redefined, or disrupted, depending on where leaders lead and the culture they have entered. Leaders who determine culture first will unearth the values that are currently upheld or withheld. As a result, they will more easily be able to craft next steps for improved culture.

How to Measure Culture

Maintaining effective culture means constantly building on the beliefs, mindsets, behaviors, and narratives within a school, district, board, or classroom. Too often, schools try to align culture through fidelity of action in curricula, pedagogical practices, or statements void of value and action. There is no accurate assessment of culture through this kind of pursuit, because a metric such as the number of staff members using a new software or curriculum shows only compliance.

I measured the effect of cultures by how trusted and supported my staff members felt, how we discussed challenges as freely as we did successes, and how willing staff members were to jump in and support our common cause (what I call the ring of fire metric, but figuratively, of course).

Culture curation is not easy. There will always be the obstacles of time (never enough), demands (often competing), and initiatives (always too many). Plus, the reasoning and practice of culture curation is hardly taught, if at all, in leadership prep courses. It's ultimately up to the leader to arrive at culture curation in a uniquely individual way.

When leaders don't recognize the need for collective culture curation, you'll end up with disheartening data and discouraging results. As a building leader in Waltham Public Schools, I worked for four superintendents in five years. The final superintendent gave district leadership a survey at our first quarterly administrative meeting and then shared the results at our next. Not surprisingly, only 44 percent of leaders said they trusted more than one person in the room. This should have been the basis for discussing the whys and setting the foundation for greater trust—an opportunity for the superintendent to curate culture. Instead, she moved on to the next survey prompt.

Surviving "Culture Killers"

Cultures of compliance and resistance exist in schools everywhere, usually with some people begrudgingly following because they want to do well by students, and others refusing to follow for the same reasons. I certainly have had this experience. The last three schools I led had experienced these "culture killers" before I came in:

- One had a long-term principal who was arrested for drunk driving a few days before school started. An interim, part-time principal filled in for two years, while also serving as the district's assistant superintendent.
- One had experienced a divisive few years, starting with a poor working relationship between the principal and assistant principal, in which sides were taken by staff members. Ultimately, a coach was hired to help build trust in the team.
- One had its principal begin a "shared" role with another school, located far across town. Things became so fraught that staff member disagreements eventually were reported in the local newspaper.

All three of those troubled schools had in them the makings of a better school, because they had at least some people who were willing to do the hard work of building or rebuilding the conditions and culture for growth and learning. All three also had the trappings of a dysfunctional culture. Staff members had survived dark days through informal pathways, where culture was created by those willing to fill the void, but who also had a willingness to buck the leadership that had let them down.

The Value of Play

One effort to build belonginess and culture with my staff members was to have them play games. This allowed educators to let their guards down and lose themselves in a task, giving them the opportunity to learn something important about each other along the way. A favorite saying of mine is "We remember what we play."

Although it wasn't the point of my coaching sessions with Lisa Votaw, principal of Aiken High School in Cincinnati, somehow she came up with an activity that she said changed her school culture for the better. In our ninety-minute coaching sessions, we often discussed challenges and triumphs, while probing how she could help her entire staff to adopt and act on a growth mindset approach to learning.

I was surprised when she told me a community scavenger hunt proved to be a game worth playing. Votaw's goals in playing were to get her staff members into the community to learn its history, landmarks, and culture and for teachers just to take a breath and have fun. Her goals were accomplished, but, incredibly the camaraderie the half-day event brought to her staff members went above and beyond what Votaw expected. Throughout the hunt, team members had ample time away from the stresses of school to share their lives with teammates, whether they knew them previously or not, and shine competitively and cooperatively. The point wasn't to win but to begin forming a culture outside the school walls that was then brought back inside.

Leading Culture, Creating Change

Leaders mindful of weak or destructive culture know there are ways to correct course over time. Those most hurt by unhealthy culture are watching and waiting for leadership missteps. In this way, leadership is not for the faint of heart or those lacking the headspace to devote to the challenges and the opportunities that lie ahead.

At its essence, culture curation is about creating a place where all people feel a sense of belongingness and know they have a place at the collective table to share their voice. As I close this chapter, the ideas behind cultures and their importance will inform a further explanation of how everyone in the educational community can rise to the challenges of inclusion in order to meet the needs of all students.

Reflections on How Life Should Be

- If leaders are to lead with their heads and their hearts, it's critical that they intentionally curate the culture from their position of power.
- Leaders who determine culture first will unearth the values that are currently upheld or withheld; then they can craft next steps for improved culture.
- The mindsets of those you lead are never as important as the mindset you hold about them. A leader's mindset matters most, not because you're the leader but because your understanding and estimation of your followers will influence their behavior and actions.
- Remain aware that culture curation is a never-ending endeavor.
- Strong cultures exist when all people feel as if they belong, have a voice, and are supported.

All Means All

I was standing in the parking lot of the Fiske Elementary School, ten feet from the school doors. I could see a second-grade boy curled up in the back seat of a school van, fast asleep. It was the end of his school day but also the beginning of a new chapter in his school life.

Sammy (student names throughout the book have been changed to protect their privacy), now safely sleeping, wasn't my son, but I loved him almost as if he were. It was with equal measures of pride, hope, and apprehension that I gently tapped on the van window. He was wrapped around his bookbag, leaning into his seatbelt, and gently snoring.

Our individual journeys to this parking lot had been separated by race, class, and age, but they were also connected by the past two years, when we had gotten to know each other. He was one of the 350 children I was responsible for each school day. Technically, he wasn't my student any longer. Sammy's mood swings had proven to be too quick, and his outbursts too consistently inconsistent, for our school to be able to respond to and resolve effectively.

Today had been his first day at an out-of-school placement, which was located several communities away. But because I empathized with him and his family's circumstance, and yes, because I loved him, I was standing here waiting to escort Sammy to his after-school program at the Fiske School. I wanted him to know that we were awaiting his arrival back to a community that believed in him and wouldn't give up on him, even if we couldn't best serve him during the school day.

All Means All—The Origin Story

When I think of all students mattering, Sammy's face is usually the first one that comes to mind because his window of opportunity of learning and growing was potentially narrowing based on so many factors out of his control; he was under ten years old when I knew him. Coy smile and lover of spiders, poetry, and his chihuahua. Short in stature but big in presence and sometimes in his demands for attention. Learning was not easy for him, but the hard work he and our team put in still influences my understanding of how to help *all* children, especially the ones who need our support, understanding, and empathy the most.

Over the years, I've continued to think of Sammy as I encountered other students who bit, kicked, threw, ran, overturned furniture in classrooms, and called me every name in the book. Although I never wanted to sustain an injury, I knew the pain inflicted by my students was not completely intended for me. It was their way of communicating hidden needs by acting out in ways that were outside the social norms at school.

My colleague, Dr. Tyrone Howard, Associate Dean for Equity & Inclusion, Graduate School of Education and Information Studies at UCLA, says, "All behavior is communication."[1] Unfortunately, too many schools treat the behavior and don't seek to "hear" what students are trying to communicate. My job was to help determine these students' needs and to fashion remedies of support for them, in addition to addressing behaviors.

Creating those remedies requires your head to research students' lives, diagnoses, and medications, relying on the expertise of the adults in school and students' outside supports of family, doctors, and mental health teams. It also takes heart in knowing the moment of pain the students inflicted on me (being punched in the chest, having my finger kicked out of joint, or being called awful names) was only temporary, and that the interaction, in fact, was never about me.

The Opportunity of the Challenging Student

Any time an episode like this happened to me, students received forgiveness and always started with a clean slate the next moment, class, or day. I have never seen value in a leadership style that seeks consequences or retribution for behaviors.

I purposely and personally invested myself in all our students' lives, but especially in the lives of the most challenging members of our community. I would join staff members in analyzing the complexity of those lives and how they affected the students' abilities to learn. We often talked about how kids were like a puzzle that needed adults to identify the missing pieces, learn where to locate them, and effectively put them into place to create a more complete picture.

If you've taken a similar route in helping your students, those seeds of seeing the value in investing in the most challenging students started somewhere. Maybe it was a recent mentor, who gave you the words to use or modeled the behaviors most likely to lead to success. Or you could have been guided by wisdom from the mouths of your students. For me, it started with a basketball program my father founded.

The Story of Shoot Straight

When I consider the foundational value I hold as an educator, it's that all students can learn, and that all means *all*. This bedrock principle first evolved early in my life through Shoot Straight, a basketball program my father, Joe Colannino, and his friend, Mike Jarvis, started together in 1978. It was designed for kids ages eight to eighteen to help them learn the fundamentals of basketball and sportsmanship, with an emphasis on learning and fun. It was innovative and far ahead of its time in many ways:

- Boys and girls played together.
- Smaller basketballs fit kids' smaller hands. ·
- Backboards were lowered to eight-and-a-half feet and hung from existing ten-foot hoops, so players could learn shooting from a basket within their reach.
- Before games, all players completed a series of drills that were tested in the first week and ultimately would be tested again at the conclusion of the ten-week program. This pre- and posttest scorecard enabled players to see improvements in shooting, dribbling, and passing.
- Teams were created from those early skills tests, so players with similar abilities played against each other, ensuring equity and the opportunity to effectively use skills learned during practice.
- Players not on the court stood along the sidelines and were active, because on-court players could pass to their off-court mates, keeping everyone involved.

It's important to note that this program happened long before widespread adjustable basketball hoops even existed, before women's basketball grew to a professional sport, and before the NCAA Division I basketball tournament became a multibillion-dollar industry. Another hallmark of the program was the inclusion of all kids playing together, no matter their race, class, gender, or abilities. Every kid who wanted to learn to play basketball was given an opportunity to do so.

For a kid like me, who grew up in a predominantly white suburb of Massachusetts, it gave me a connection to basketball players from diverse communities such as Cambridge, Boston, Fall River, and New Bedford. The program had a profound and lasting impact on me, even though my future as a pro athlete was hampered by the fact that I never grew taller than five feet seven inches.

Shoot Straight began as a winter program, but it soon added a summer camp, too. Now I was living, sleeping, and eating with these kids who all loved basketball as much as I did. We had that in common, but we also began to learn about and share our music, food, and worldviews with one another.

I will always be indebted to my dad and Mike for creating something that informed not only my basketball playing but also my understanding of life beyond Woburn, Massachusetts, which was a small, working-class, homogenous city. I grew up with the mostly white sons and daughters of electricians, teachers, bartenders, and nurses. Through Shoot Straight, I met and made friends with kids of all colors and backgrounds. Because I laughed, succeeded, and failed along with them, I became a person with a wider, more inclusive, worldview.

My father believed not only in all kids' abilities to learn basketball but also that they could learn something about themselves. This meant that all were welcome, including children with physical, emotional, and cognitive disabilities. We cheered for players who had to overcome physical and mental obstacles just to hold, dribble, pass, and shoot a basketball, whether they were on our team or not. Seeing them try and prevail raised the spirits of the child who struggled and those who witnessed the child's perseverance.

Acceptance and Accommodation

When leaders think of "all students," they should include those who have the most trouble learning or functioning within the norms of school. No student willingly wants to fail or be seen as an "other" that doesn't belong in class with their peers, even though they sometimes behave this way. What goes unseen are the experiences and feelings that aren't shared by students that can lead up to outbursts or behaviors outside school norms.

If we dismiss these toughest students, believe that making plans to assist them is a waste of time, or can't wait to move them out of a class, school, or district, then we've fallen short of our ultimate goal as educators. Beyond causing these students further harm, the school and community are robbed of the potential maturing students can provide when they learn and grow.

Today and Tomorrow

Today. Define what *all* means in your class, department, school, or district. In doing so, leaders cannot simply disregard students who are struggling academically, socially, or emotionally. It's likely that there are adults who are failing children in your schools because they do not yet possess the disposition, skills, or strategies to help all students. Find and amplify those staff members who succeed with all students and model what it means to really support all kids.

Tomorrow. Create response-to-intervention teams not only for academic challenges but also for those social and emotional challenges that often precede low achievement. Make discrete and measurable goals such as improving grades and learning through reteaching and retakes of tests; creating pathways for underserved populations such as multilingual learners, special education (SPED), and Black and Brown kids into gifted and talented programming and advanced placement classes; as well the supports needed for them to become successful. Your measures of improved access can include everything from percentages of historically underserved populations taking upper level courses to alumni entering the professions of their passions.

Inclusion for all cannot coexist with exclusionary beliefs that eliminate *all* and replace it with *some*. You may have the most wonderfully written mission and vision statements prominently framed and hung on school walls, but once you exclude a student, the words are at best disingenuous and at worst hypocritical.

If educators support inclusion (and all schools should), then they must look deeply into how their systems work with and support those who need accommodations, modifications, and caring adults present. A first step is simply to accept children for who they are, imperfect and in need of receiving the skills and strategies that will lead to greater success and a sense of belonging. For some kids, this means teaching them how to sit in their seat, transition from lunch, ask for help, or begin to study. If you've been in a classroom for just a few weeks, you can relate to my oft-repeated adage that you have to teach your students *everything*, even something as mundane but necessary as how to blow their nose with a tissue. (Back when I was a classroom teacher, it once took me all year, but I did finally teach a particularly challenging student how to do this!)

Sammy's Story: Skill, Not Will

Let's go back to the parking lot for a minute, where I'm watching Sammy sleep. His skill set was weak, not because he couldn't learn, but because of circumstances outside his control. It was the duty and honor of the adults in school to be clear, specific, empathetic, and encouraging so Sammy could attain basic skills taken for granted by other students, such as raising a hand to ask a question, checking with a classmate for understanding, or getting ready to transition from one activity to the next.

Sammy needed a significant number of accommodations and modifications, as spelled out in his individual education plan (IEP). By the time he turned six, his student file was several inches thick. Our school psychologist, Sharon Grossman, and I had first met with him and his mother the summer before he was to start first grade with us.

Sammy's mom told us of his lack of success in kindergarten and how he had been sent home countless times because of emotional outbursts. Through his IEP, we could see his diagnosis and disabilities, including post-traumatic stress disorder (PTSD). His mom explained that Sammy had witnessed domestic violence from his father toward her for his entire early life. To put the impact of that situation into context, consider the milestones children reach from birth to five years of age—walking, talking, sharing emotions, toilet training, and acquiring early literacy skills. Then imagine how those milestones would be impeded by constant reactions to stress and violence during those crucial developmental times. A child's brain actually becomes malformed through traumatic stress.[2] As the child matures, typical reactions to everyday occurrences are replaced with fight, flight, or freeze, because the brain's traumatic response is always on, trying to protect itself from harm.

In that early meeting, we promised Sammy's mom we would do everything we could to keep him learning in school. We met with Sammy's teacher and shared plans of support. Sharon and I pledged our presence to be by Sammy's side, beyond his mandated IEP services, working to build positive relationships with him. This meant a whole host of times we'd just drop in to see how Sammy was doing, pulling him aside to read poetry or just talk to him. We had to let him know that he could trust us, even if he made mistakes or acted out. As long as he wasn't putting himself, classmates, or teachers in danger, he would stay in school for the entire day, even on a day when he had multiple outbursts. At those times, he debriefed with Sharon or me, reviewed the mistakes he may have made, and discussed a self-identified skill he would work on for the rest of the day.

This was hard work behaviorally, academically, and socially for Sammy, and it was hard work for all the adults supporting him, too. Behavior modification plans—providing discrete and limited social skills he could attain and be rewarded for—were in constant motion and in need of revision. His special education teacher, as well as Sharon and I, were consistently called on to help support his classroom teacher and would sometimes have to remove him from class to deescalate, reflect, and build skills for a return to class. We rarely sent him home, because he wasn't destructive or hurtful to others. But he *was* missing the skills needed to deal with typical changes in a school day and required our reinforcement and encouragement to help him get through each day.

The Power of Noticing

I learned to follow up my debriefs with Sammy by walking him into class and praising him a specific way, which had a calming and encouraging effect on him. I would grab a first-grade chair, sit next to him, whisper what I observed he was doing to be a member of the class. I began each statement with the words "I noticed." A typical return to class after an outburst sounded like this:

- "I noticed you sat in your seat without disrupting the class or teacher."
- "I noticed you found and took out your materials so you could participate."
- "I noticed you raised your hand to ask your teacher where the class is in the lesson."

There's power in noticing, especially for students like Sammy, who frequently experience substantial failure in school, are reprimanded for it, and who then are embarrassed by their lack of success. Once a pattern of frustration between student and teacher sets in, most praise becomes useless because (1) the student won't believe the positive praise after being overcome with consistent negative attention and redirection and (2) the student resists feedback correcting behaviors as a matter of self-worth because the student feels the need to fight the negative perception from a steady stream of adult interaction that feels or is negative.

With students such as Sammy, simply noticing behaviors provided him with the power and control to determine the praise's worth.[3] There is no value judgment in noticing what a student is doing. It's simply reporting what is observed. But negative value is communicated in the following feedback, the tone of voice that is used, and a teacher's body language, which struggling students like Sammy can become hyper-focused on.

- "Sit down."
- "Stop talking."
- "We're not supposed to have our crayons out now."
- "You need to pay attention."
- "Stop tapping your pencil."
- "Make better choices."
- "Why are you disrupting the class again?"

After a few times of saying "I noticed" to Sammy, he asked me to write the feedback down. Using sticky notes in addition to verbal feedback gave Sammy the opportunity to reference my praise when I wasn't available, which enabled him to determine the skills that would help him learn on his own.

Too often children like Sammy, whether or not they have a diagnosis or disability, are seen as willful children unwilling to cooperate and integrate themselves into the school day. Sharon taught me and our Fiske School staff an important way of looking at these children by the phrase, "It's skill, not will."

Once we addressed Sammy's behaviors as skills and outlined the strategies that he needed to attain those skills, it was like teaching any other subject. In this case, though, Sammy's skill attainment would enable him to function better in his classroom so he could learn the content. Unfortunately, frustrated and under-supported educators can shift the responsibility for teaching such a challenging child by labeling them as "willful." When multiple children with these challenges are present, it can feel impossible to teach an entire class while spending lots of time admonishing children who are seen as being purposely disruptive.

Modeling *All* with Staff Members

Teachers lacking support or experience can easily fall back on just a few standardized responses for all students. This is detrimental to helping students learn and a disrespectful disservice to them, especially those who struggle. Teachers can unwittingly or intentionally teach to the middle of their classes for efficiency and effectiveness. In districts with specialized teaching resources, teachers and leaders can hand the responsibility of reaching challenging students to departments that act like detached learning silos, including Title 1, multilingual learning, SPED, behavioral programs, and alternative high schools.

It's a dilemma many schools face—having a wide array of teachers who should help students learn in general education classes in conjunction, collaboration, and consultation with general education teachers. This sometimes results in a downloading of responsibility to teachers with specialized expertise, in which they hold the sole responsibility for teaching. I observed it, for example, when a first-grade teacher passed the buck to the multilingual educator to teach their shared, French-speaking students how to read.

Leaders have the chance to serve all students by developing more comprehensive, collaborative, and cohesive education teams. This requires creating the means—the time and availability to meet and share strategies that work in multiple settings—so students are consistently reinforced in their learning regardless of where and with whom the learning happens.

Mindset Moment

I've been conducting professional development workshops for more than six years, and I've learned that, no matter where I go, there will always be skeptics. Once, at the conclusion of a session on using encouraging, growth-minded language, an obviously skeptical teacher asked these questions:

Teacher: Sure, this is all great, but how am I supposed "encourage" a student who takes a test and just writes his name at the top of the page and leaves the rest of it blank? What do you say to a blank test?

Me: Did you ask the student why he didn't complete the test?

Teacher: No.

Me: I'd start there.

When we aren't curious about students' attitudes, beliefs, obstacles, or performance, we tell them we will accept a lack of effort, and we let them know that we aren't interested in why or what's getting in their way.

Teachers want the best for their students but can stumble when called on to respond to behaviors outside their expertise. Whether they're attempting to reach twenty-four second graders or more than one hundred students in four sections of freshman English, teachers already are faced with daunting tasks that require differentiation across their classes. In many classes, even those that are tracked in middle and high schools, students have varying levels of understanding and skill levels. Teachers can bemoan this fact or take action by teaching the skills necessary for each student, wherever he or she stands on the learning continuum. From those who need reteaching with direct teacher instruction to those who can independently seek and solve more challenging material, teachers need to provide what children need, when they need it.

It's also unfair to saddle teachers with the sole responsibility for responding to challenges of equity, disabilities, second language, and behavior while also expecting content to be delivered. Just like students, adults need skills, strategies, and learning that help them frame, respond, plan, and access how they are doing in meeting the needs of all their students.

Adults Practicing Separation

Educators must also see their leaders model inclusion with their staff members, students, and families. To light a path for everyone else, building leaders, curriculum heads, and those providing direct service must work together through the challenges of inclusion and take time for cross-curricula, department, or grade-level meetings, planning, and follow-through.

That's not to say that this kind of coworking model is easy to achieve, because it isn't. There are formal and informal difficulties with working together in schools, starting with delineations between departments, curricula, and even what is valued. Leaders and teachers encounter these separations of power and control just about any time they want to innovate and collaborate based on data, research, or pedagogical practice.

Siloing, Multilingual Learners, and Me

I remember a time I wanted to provide the same level of reading instruction support given to general education teachers for those teaching multilingual learners, but I was told by the director of reading that multilingual students already had their own literacy programming. The problem was that the multilingual staff members did not have the same level of support. They had practices of sheltered English immersion, not the guided reading practices and professional development afforded general education staff members. An inequity was exposed within my school, and I wanted to remedy it by including multilingual teachers in all our professional development.

I was already a building leader, but crossing this divide was much more difficult than I thought it would be. I uncovered a gap constricted by the dangers of ego, ignorance, and possessiveness. School district leadership structure that prizes individual expertise by content area and grade level runs in opposition to cultivating new ways of thinking collectively across grades, content areas, or schools. Because central office leaders had such an aversion to collaborating just about everywhere I taught or led, I would either have to convince them my idea was their idea or request a pilot program with a beginning and end date so as not to disrupt the guarded spaces of individual expertise. And, yes, it was exhausting.

Defining Differences as Opportunities

Daily expectations, such as paying attention, completing work/assignments, studying for tests, behaving according to written and unwritten rules, and participating in all aspects of school life, can fall away when students don't feel included, loved, cared for, and validated, regardless of their status socially, academically, and emotionally. It worsens the effect when educators, in conference and teacher rooms, use labels such as *lazy, troublemaker,* or *defiant.*

All means ensuring universal inclusion. If schools shut students out by not resolving the difficult circumstances of learning that some students present, we are telling and showing children that they don't matter to us. The education process becomes corrupted through bias, stereotype, and prejudice, coupled with lack of vision and support for teachers to accept and see differences in their students as opportunities.

Instead of understanding individuals and groups more deeply, we slap students with reported labels of difference—African American, Asian, at-risk, poor, and so on—which can serve only as categories to fit students in, not for adults to better understand cultural differences. Even students without external categorizations, such as those who are witnesses of domestic abuse, sufferers of the effects of alcoholism, or those uncertain about their sexuality, become filled with dread for school because they feel as though they do not belong.

Inclusion is about belongingness, a value that must be codified systematically through educator and student discovery about student interests, talents, perspectives, and experiences and how those can be correlated and connected through a meaningful curriculum, in part, tailored to need. This can and does happen all across the curriculum by educators and leaders who believe in students and who see possibilities where others see natural obstacles.

The Calculus Project

Dr. Adrian Mims, my colleague and friend, has dedicated his life to understanding how race and class determine why Black and Brown high school students often are excluded from advanced placement (AP) math classes or fail rapidly and withdraw into lower-level courses. Adrian is an imposing figure at six feet two inches tall. I noticed this while sitting next to him during our first education leadership class together—me fitting comfortably in the attached chair-desk combination filling colleges across the country and built for someone my size and him stretching out well beyond the confines of our seats. His easygoing disposition and thoughtful approach to challenges belie his commanding physical presence. He's also Black and from South Carolina, the two of us separated by thousands of miles, climates, and cultures.

While working as dean of Brookline High School, a mostly affluent school district neighboring Boston, Adrian noticed a disheartening fact when following twenty Black students who had started in AP geometry during their freshman year. By senior year, there were only a couple of Black students in AP calculus. When Adrian asked students why they dropped the class, they provided these responses:

- "I was the only Black kid in my class, and I felt responsible for my whole race."
- "Black kids obviously don't belong in advanced placement math classes."
- "After I did poorly first term, the teacher recommended I drop the class."

From this dire situation, The Calculus Project was born, in which Adrian would recognize rising Black and Brown eighth graders to seniors with the hopes of supporting them as they matriculated all the way through AP calculus. The program provided prelearning for an upcoming math course during a four-week summer class, identified fellow classmates and teachers as mentors, communicated and supported greater parental involvement, and grouped Black and Brown students in sizable cohorts in honors and advanced classes during the school year.

The Calculus Project, which is still going strong, holds all students, parents, and educators accountable for believing that children of color can excel in advanced math. That's not an easy task when challenges of beliefs, mindsets, behaviors, and narratives don't always mesh with a need to work through ignorance. When Adrian was formalizing the first year of the program and asked the math department to group a critical mass of Black students in honors and advanced levels, he was rejected by the department chair. Teachers felt uncomfortable with cohorts of Black students in their classes.

Fortunately, Adrian found two math teachers willing to volunteer to accept cohorts of Black students. Just two years after the program's inception, 53 percent of Black students at Brookline High School scored advanced in the state's tenth-grade math test. Before The Calculus Project, just 18 percent of Black students scored advanced.[4]

"Companies already are actively recruiting engineers from other countries to come to the United States to work," Mims says. "Here we are, with students who have the abilities to become engineers and fill all kinds of careers related to math, and we're overlooking them based on race and gender. They're right here in our classes waiting for us, if we'd only support them better."

The Impact of Teachers' Views

"All meaning all" is a concept even larger than equity, because it's actually what we do for ourselves and helping students become whatever they want to become. Self-actualization should ultimately be the goal of all schools. When I started teaching fifth grade in 1998 at Boston's Agassiz Elementary School, I told my class that I hoped to help them discover something in themselves that would make them successful in their lives, even though they were only ten- and eleven-year-olds at the time.

The school's makeup was 100 percent poverty, greater than 75 percent multilingual learners, and mostly Black and Brown faces staring back at me. Still, I meant what I said and said I what I meant! Among that first group of fifth graders, there now is a practicing attorney and another who is a medical student. Even if I played just a small part in their success, that's enough for me.

Education researcher John Hattie has risen to prominence by analyzing the greatest influencers on a children's learning through curricula, student experience, home life, school, classroom, teacher, and teaching practices. There are currently 252 influences of Hattie's Visible Learning that he has categorized, from those most hurtful (retaining students) to those most helpful (collective teacher efficacy). Among those with the greatest effect on student learning is a "teacher's estimate of achievement," which refers to teachers' belief in all students' ability to learn, regardless of circumstances.[5]

A large part of this starts with the beliefs of teachers, schools, and systems about whether or not a student belongs with them. If students don't look, act, behave, respond, or acquiesce to a teacher's or a school's standards and norms, whole groups of students can be regarded as "nonlearners."

Student validation comes first through adults being willing to understand students through relationship-building, interest inventories, and surveying them on learning styles, struggles, and successes. This is another step in making culture curation helpful—providing worth for all, but especially for those outside or challenging the norms of school. Simply providing an opportunity for students to showcase what they know or who they are in class, school, and district promotes the sacred American individualist ethos, but more importantly provides a level of acceptance from truly knowing someone else, where they come from, how they learn, and what they're passionate about.

Back to Sammy

At the Fiske School, we knew Sammy. We never gave up on him, even when his special education team and his mom decided that, given Sammy's intensifying needs, we could not best provide the proper level of services and expertise at our school. It hurt me to agree that "yes, Sammy needs more than us."

But because Sammy's third-party after-school program was housed at Fiske, I made sure he arrived back at our school at the end of every school day. He came back to a place that still loved and accepted him for who he was, even though we were now playing a smaller role in helping him learn and grow. That's why I found myself standing there, staring down at him and gently tapping on the van window. Sammy eventually shook off his sleep, and we walked the ten feet into school together.

That's how it went, every single school day. We talked about the weekend, his favorite candy, a book he was reading, or anything on his mind. Briefly, but importantly, we continued the relationship begun two years previously.

Leaders Create Bridges

I was creating a ten-foot bridge each day by walking Sammy into our school from the van. It didn't matter that the van driver and the after-school company had refused to walk him to the school door. It mattered more that I said I would. Eventually school staff members noticed my daily duty and offered to help, too. In this way, Sammy became more than just my responsibility; he became the responsibility of our entire school community.

There's a heartwarming coda to this story: I bumped into Sammy at a local fair a few years ago when he was in fifth grade. From a few feet away,

Sammy's mom and I saw each other first, and we both began to cry, as we came in for a hug. Our hearts were full in recognition of where we'd been and the lengths we had gone in hopes of widening the window of success for Sammy. Although Sammy had made some gains socially and emotionally, his academic challenges continued. He looked well as we talked briefly and posed for a picture, one I keep in my phone to this day.

Sometimes the bridge is only ten feet; sometimes it feels like ten miles. But building these bridges is based on a hope that we can see and get to what's beyond us. And when we work to include all, we will find ways to share love with all members of our educational community, as I'll explore in chapter 3.

Reflections on How Life Should Be

- Be willing to invest your head and heart in your most challenging students.
- Use the power of noticing to draw your attention to will, not skill.
- What I learned from Shoot Straight, my dad's basketball program: Play together, make accommodations, and include everyone.
- What I learned from The Calculus Project for Black and Brown students: The next generation of talent is already here in our classrooms, waiting only for our acknowledgment and support.
- If your central office is balking at a new way of collaboratively working, try convincing them it was their idea or request a pilot program with beginning and end dates.

3

Love

Because leaders don't gather around conference tables or hold faculty meetings to talk about how they love their work, colleagues, staff, mission, and, most importantly, their students, this chapter will stand out from the rest. With absence comes a void that needs to be defined and filled for further reflection, discussion, and action. A goal of my leadership has been to make anyone I was leading feel special in my presence, and this takes healthy amounts of love, which leads to empathy, understanding, compassion, and dignity.

Love is a four-letter word. You'd think from its marked absence from public education discourse that it actually belongs with a list of dirty words not allowed in schools, instead of being the driving force behind growth and change.

From Shakespeare's sonnets to holy texts to every genre of music, we delight in sharing and hearing of love's lasting impact, its joys of discovery, or sorrows when it is lost. One of my favorite jazz standards, "Nature Boy," extolls the cyclical nature of love—stating that whatever love is given ultimately becomes a love returned.

Schools are a natural place to give and receive love because being there offers many chances to share in this life-altering emotion for children and adults alike. And schools have the ability and opportunity to change lives. I used to tell my staff members, "If you change just one life for the better throughout your career, you have changed the course of humanity forever due to all the lives that one life will touch." School is the place, and love is the emotion that ultimately enables educators to improve their students' immediate todays and future tomorrows.

A leader who expresses love has the power to amplify its positive effects when love is acknowledged, made a basis for decision-making, and modeled for all to see. Leaders can't just use the words; they have to act on them.

The apprehension about love in leading is understandable and peculiar. Leaders who seek out opportunities to share their love, passion for teaching, and learning with those they lead are able to break through the awkwardness that permeates so many leadership teams because they fail to even consider expressing love. Leaders may also wonder how love can be on the table when schools suffer from varied and urgent challenges such as low achievement, overactive or disengaged parents, underfunding, or inequities in need of responses. Infusing the pedagogy, curriculum, and policies with love would better serve all.[1] Leaders who are impassioned to serve those they lead will not allow obstacles to stop all from learning because love of the process, delivery, and assessment of learning also is a message of hope and optimism.

Love in Action

If you recall Cleburne ISD in chapter 1, passion is one of the district's core values. They further define this as "love what you do." Dr. Heath says the staff members were challenged when they first tackled this value. "Defining what you truly love is not easy sometimes and may not match with your current role. Loving what you do should be part of everyone's daily work life because when we have this outlook, we'll look at challenges as positive opportunities to improve, grow, and love our jobs even more. If love is absent, where's the drive to meet challenges or even agree on what we should celebrate?"

At Cleburne, love is on the table, and it's evident in every facet of learning. It was clear when the district tracked all eight thousand of its students during the COVID-19 school shutdown in spring 2020. With just two students unaccounted for the district kept searching until they discovered that those students' families had moved out of the district.

This shows that it's possible for schools to address common issues such as chronic absenteeism with love, and it's a concept that can be expanded. Instead of punishing children for absences, schools could take the time, effort, and energy to find out why students are absent and work individually with each child who requires additional support. This would exemplify how it looks to love all students, no matter how disenfranchised they seem to be.

The Impact Exercise

Think of a teacher or coach who made an impact on your life. What did that person do *for* you and *to* you? Consider what in that person's approach went

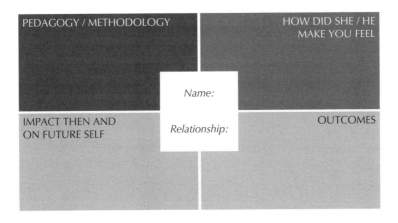

FIGURE 3.1   An Educator's Impact

beyond the content, activity, or sport he or she was charged with teaching. How did that person affect you then, when you were a student, or now, as an adult and educator?

When you do think about that educator, you'll likely go through many memories and feelings. There are many ways to change and grow, but certainly as an impressionable student, love from an adult who took an interest in you is a powerful driver for growth. Author James Baldwin said, "If I love you, I have to make you conscious of the things you don't see."[2] Teachers who see their students' futures, do so with love in their hearts, along with the methods to form impactful relationships in the present, so students can become whatever they want, especially when they don't yet see what they can be.

When I make presentations to groups of educators, I walk them through the "impactor" graphic shown in Figure 3.1. It enables teachers and leaders to consider exactly how an adult affected them. For my example, I use my favorite high school English teacher, Ms. Nancy Leverich. This is how she changed my life:

- *Pedagogy/methodology.* Used the Socratic method relentlessly, asking us questions on how power is used and abused while teaching books such as *1984*, *One Flew Over the Cuckoo's Nest*, and *I Am the Cheese.*
- *How did she make me feel.* Like I belonged because my opinion mattered and, thus, I mattered.

- *Impact then and on future self.* I considered how individuals and governments use or abuse their power and for what gain was that power used. I made sure I considered my power when I held it over students and staff members.
- *Outcomes.* With whatever power I have had, I have tried to empower others.

Ms. Leverich taught me during the 1985–1986 school year, and yet I carry her lessons into my current life of teaching, leading, consulting, and writing. She was also the only teacher I allowed to sign my high school yearbook.

Love can be evidenced in most, if not everything, we do at school. A student succeeds through hard work and teacher encouragement. A colleague listens carefully to a peer's misgivings about a new curriculum. Parents thank their principal for recommending an outside therapist who helped their child through a challenge. Even when a student trashes a room, runs from his principal, and then punches him in the chest, there's an opportunity to respond with love. (See chapter 5 for the roller-coaster story of how this happened to me.) Taking a moment to provide the means to help someone understand or persevere, regardless of mistakes made, is love in play.

Leading with our hearts enables us to pause and consider best courses of action that are likely to have a positive impact on those we serve. We know that when we do the following, positive results happen:

- Provide encouragement, a child feels worthy
- Carefully listen, a colleague feels valued
- Offer assistance, a parent feels thankful

Understanding a need and fulfilling that need is a necessary action of leadership. It's actually a foundational element of leading, and it requires a great deal of empathy to see within someone else's experience and offer a helping hand. Without love there is no empathy.

Sometime during your teaching career you've likely said, "I love to teach!" If you're still teaching, I hope you continue to say it often. I'd argue that if you don't continue to list "love of teaching" as a reason for remaining in this profession, then a lack of passion will make your job significantly more challenging.

You must love to teach and to lead through the difficulties presented daily. Whether you are a classroom teacher or an administrator, you are often required to work through challenges such as these:

- Unscheduled interruptions
- A child crying in his or her seat
- The need to deliver critical feedback
- Uncertainty in how to more be equitable in instruction and curricula
- Losing school or district status due to poor standardized test results

This list could go on and on, because challenges tend to be much longer than the hours in the school day. Delivering learning is a job that's more than a demanding career. It's a calling, a distinction with a difference, and one that demands that we love to teach and learn.

Building on a Foundation of Love

If leaders give themselves permission to lead with love, there are long-ignored possibilities waiting to be explored as methods and means for improvement and change. Of course, there are the obvious signs of affection, such as high-fives, smiles, and pats on the back—literal and figurative. Educators will likely never forget how the pandemic of 2020–2021 suddenly changed how they could express love to staff members, students, families, and direct reports.

Education was required to make a major shift in March 2020, and that meant more deliberate actions and words were needed to replace the physical acts, when students and teachers were separated by shields, masks, and social distancing. Love's response was to find a new way—emoji stickers on a screen, recorded videos posted about personal triumphs or misgivings, and plenty of time to check in individually or within a class of twenty-five. Just slowing down to consider the lives of adults or children reduced to fit on a screen with just one-inch by one-inch representations of whole people was important. Teaching became immediate and intimate, with so many watching and listening within the enclosed space of a computer screen.

A New Online Reality

In a classroom, students can be seated in groups or rows, with some paying attention and others preoccupied with something other than the teacher. If a teacher admonishes a student at school, some students in close proximity will likely feel the teacher's frustration or resentment. Other students may miss it because of physical distance or their own distractibility. On a device's screen, no matter the size, every student has the opportunity to feel what any student is feeling, because although the physical distance is great, attention and emotion can be more concentrated.

With or without a camera on, students can sense a teacher's mood. Even if students are not paying attention, they have the ability to communicate within and outside learning platforms to privately discuss a teacher's actions in real time. Texting or private messaging for older students has the potential to take over a class outside the teacher's knowledge. For younger students, there's the possibility of family members listening in on a class.

Teachers who invested time empathizing, understanding, and just getting to know their students pre-COVID-19 are the same educators who, post-pandemic, students not only tuned into but also worked hard for. The old adage remained true: "Students don't care how much you know until they know how much you care." If learning, achievement, and growth are to happen, love is the first seed that has to be planted.

Meet Toney Jackson

One example is Toney Jackson of Hackensack, New Jersey. Jackson wears his abundant locs [*locs* is Toney's distinction because they are not dreadlocks] wrapped atop his head, and he teaches with an ever-present smile, sharing his love of poetry, hip-hop, and rap music with his class. When schools shut down, he opened a whole new world of distance learning by allowing his fourth-grade students to express themselves asynchronously through video creations.

During the pandemic, Jackson built a makeshift video studio in his basement. Imperfect as it was, with spotlights mounted from basement pipes and a green screen just big enough to transport Jackson wherever he wanted to go onto superimposed images, the studio became a transformative place of innovation and inspiration.

Jackson acknowledges the difficulties of teaching remotely, but he emphasizes that he was able to overcome many obstacles, and his students did, too. It took a willingness to share his imperfections with his students—less-than-professional lighting, many retakes to get a rap just right, or last-minute changes in schedule when his daughter woke up early from her naps. Jackson modeled that mistakes were OK, but his desire to stay connected with his students far outweighed whatever snafus that arose. If Jackson could work through his mistake as the teacher, his students could do the same, and they did!

At first, Jackson used a video-creation and -sharing platform as a means of introduction and connection for his students for just a couple of assignments. Students completed these assignments, showing off their rooms, homes, or interests, just so they could maintain their classroom culture, even though they were far apart. When he left further video creations up to his students to complete on their own time, the students responded eagerly. Amazingly, eighteen students created more than five hundred videos to share with one another about their lives in just four months' time.

Jackson says, "It was surprising. The videos were not assigned classwork, but students wanted to create things for each other to see. I think sometimes in the classroom you'll see that, but it was awesome to see that they had such a commitment and desire to do that while they were at home, when it was entirely optional."

The creation of space to meaningfully connect with peers in a virtual environment is an act of love because it filled a void for Jackson's students. Missing their daily in-person chances to discuss, learn, and experiment with classmates, Jackson created a safe and exciting alternative. He never asked for these personal videos, but students knew they would be welcomed, because Jackson loves his students and revels in knowing more about them.

He also opened up his world to them during the pandemic. Jackson's young daughter joined him on video lessons when he cooked, or she could be heard just off-screen when he was dressed as a Revolutionary War soldier. He made videos of himself working in his home garden and shot his video in his homemade studio. Jackson's students were presented with a model of not only what it was like to teach and learn during the pandemic but also what it meant to live your best life with those you love.

How Kent Brewer Learned to Say "I Love You"

The same can be said of leaders—teachers engaged in the difficulty of changing the methods, pedagogy, and technology of teaching with support from leaders who care first about their staff members' well-being. This sets a course of action through agreed-on values, which may or may not have been written out ahead, as was found out during the coronavirus outbreak. It's likely the leaders who showed love virtually were already doing so before school went on a pandemic hiatus. However and whenever meetings, supervision, and professional development happens, leaders who take moments to signal joy and camaraderie with their staff members receive the benefits of that joy returned.

Leaders such as Kent Brewer, elementary school principal of small-town Linton-Stockton Elementary School in Indiana, leaned on the loving culture and relationships he started creating before his schools reopened for the 2020–2021 school year. In fall 2019, Kent started ending morning announcements by saying, "If no one has told you that they love you today, please know that Mr. Brewer loves you."

Today and Tomorrow

Today. Include love in your morning message, weekly email, or simply by telling colleagues, staff members, and students what you love about them, using specific examples for classrooms to boardrooms.

Tomorrow. Healthy relationships start with love. As you move into future plans, place love prominently in your values like Cleburne ISD does. Define how educators show love to students, peers, and parents and highlight how love contributes to a happier and more productive school.

Brewer, a long-time teacher turned Title 1 director and finally an elementary school principal, had been thinking about saying "I love you" to his students and staff members for a couple years before bringing love into his daily announcements and then into other aspects of his leadership. Kent was encouraged to do this by his assistant principal, Nathan Moore. Kent mentioned that he was trying to find just the right moment to more intentionally include love into his daily leadership. Nathan said to Kent, "Today's the day to include love into your morning message as a start."

Kent was initially apprehensive about saying "I love you" on morning announcements. But now it's a phrase that can now be heard in the hallways of Linton-Stockton Elementary School, thanks to his willingness to move beyond the apprehension of his head and lead more fully with his heart. During the beginning of face-to-face learning in August 2020, Kent and Nathan walked around school and videoed each teacher teaching for about thirty seconds. Then they asked teachers whom they'd like to thank for supporting them in their return to school during an anxious time. Kent and Nathan then sent the short teacher clips as thank-you notes to each teacher's chosen loved one. In this way, Kent was sharing his love beyond school into the greater community.

"Mr. Colannino, I Love You"

On our first day of my first year as a fifth-grade teacher, our principal at the Agassiz Elementary School in Boston's Jamaica Plain neighborhood told the teachers, "You must love your students." He was right, and I was happy to hear him say it. He was, in fact, the only leader in seventeen years of public schools who ever framed love as a requirement of our work. Sadly, I found his words to be just that: words with little action to support them.

Agassiz was built during the 1970s open concept movement. Three classrooms were clustered together sharing a small hallway. Every room also shared a movable wall separating them, which could be folded accordion-style, with the room on the ends able to open up to the middle classroom to create larger learning spaces and shared teaching opportunities. The idea was to enable teachers to teach into each other's classrooms. (I never opened my movable wall and never heard of anyone else doing so twenty-five years after the school was constructed.) The back wall of these classes was actually the shared hallway, so the plan was open indeed. In my cluster of three teachers, the music room was set between my class and a fourth-grade multilingual classroom. The kids walked in the hallway—really the back of my room—all day long on their way to and from the music room.

It was not the best environment in which to teach and learn. It was easy to be distracted by teacher and student voices spilling over into each other's classroom, in addition to the music that played during the music instruction parts of the day. Worse, there was just one window in each classroom. The scuttlebutt from the mostly veteran staff members was that the school was built without windows, and the teachers' union had to fight to receive one long, narrow window per classroom.

From the outside, the school looked like a concrete prison. Inside, the adults pulled together into cliques, refusing to talk with one another. More than three-quarters of our students were native Spanish speakers, primarily first- or second-generation immigrants from Central and South American countries. Our one-hundred-person teaching staff mirrored our students, with 75 percent of classes led by teachers with multilingual expertise. The rest of classes, like mine, were taught to native English speakers and multilingual students who had progressed enough to be in an English-only classroom. The classes became more comingled as students matured and received their specialized instruction. The two groups of teachers did not follow the children's example and only mixed or mingled during special occasions such as staff member retirement parties.

We didn't even eat lunch together with multilingual teachers, who ate downstairs next to the office. The rest of us ate in the third-floor library. I usually did, too, after trying to sit with my multilingual colleagues a few times on the first floor. I didn't feel welcome and most staff members spoke Spanish during their lunch break, which I didn't understand.

When I offered to run a teacher's reading group for staff members, my proposal was met with cynical whispers. "That will never happen" and "Why would you want to do *that*?" I worried that only a fraction of teachers would sign up to take part in something fun. I moved forward anyway, inviting teachers and the principal to meet monthly to discuss books we'd read. I was hoping to re-create what were supposed to do with students during our literacy classes—build excitement on shared reading experiences.

As part of our literacy programming, every teacher taught students different from their homeroom class across grade levels and at different reading levels. For instance, I was a fifth-grade teacher, but for ninety minutes each day I taught second-, third- and fourth-grade students on a third-grade reading level. I was hoping to mirror this varied mix of students by meeting with a cross-section of teachers in a book club format.

Our ten-person group met after school at a local bar to discuss a common book read. We met infrequently, but we did enjoy each other's company when we met. The apprehension to join together was real, and I was unable to pull more teachers together despite my best intentions. It occurred to me that the principal wanted us to love our students, but we didn't even love ourselves. I left the Agassiz the following year and the book club was dropped after that.

With little action behind the principal's words to model and show us all what it meant to love students and, thus, love staff members, we mostly stayed within groups based on whom we taught. I don't know if it was the demands of the job, his years on the job, or the widespread poverty of our students, but there were few examples of love in action, even though our principal demanded we love our students.

Mindset Moment

During my first principal job, some of my students didn't have parents who were willing or able to attend back-to-school night. I offered to plant potted daffodils with any student who wanted to attend the event without a parent.

One group of fourth-grade girls showed up without their parents. As we worked, one of the girls stood on her tiptoes behind me and whispered, "Mr. Colannino, I love you." At that point in my career, I hadn't expected such an expression of thanks, but as I continued to lead, I learned that often my students, staff members, and parents would share their love of our love-focused school culture with me.

I knew I loved my students, so much so that my first official act as their teacher was to wash the disgustingly dirty walls of our classroom a few days before school started. The ten-foot-high cinderblock walls looked as if they hadn't been washed in years. It took a ladder, a mop, lots of soap and water, and great effort, but it was ultimately worth it. Clean walls were a sign of love as clear as the interest, enthusiasm, and passion of my teaching. Love doesn't have to be played like a blaring a horn from your office, but it does take intentionality in delivery.

Students and teachers will rally and respond to any adversity or challenge if they know they are loved. This begets a sense of safety and belongingness. Love from leaders and educators lets those we lead and teach know that "you can screw up and it will be all right." It creates an environment where everyone can succeed and flourish, even as we wait patiently for the wounded, the cynical, or the angry to come along. Love knows we are far from perfect and doesn't even expect perfection. It lays the foundation for effort, mutual respect, dignity, and joy.

The Pineapples, the Underwear, and the Effective Leader

When I was nearing my departure from the MacArthur Elementary School in Waltham, Massachusetts, after five years as a principal, a veteran teacher said to me, "Anthony, you always seem to be around when I need you. How do you do that?"

Love is more than words; it's working with all those you lead with a heart that aligns a warmth for fellow educators with a head willing to take the necessary steps to act on it. This starts with a leader's own reflection on actions and reactions. Are you speaking with anger, disappointment, or impatience, especially when misunderstandings arise? What's your stance or body language? Where is the love? If love is absent, and it easily can be due to challenges that arise daily, those you lead will know. I didn't do anything special to be recognized by one of my teachers except being visible and available whenever necessary.

Because conflict is inherent in leading, no matter which job you hold, we should ask ourselves, "How am I acting?" If self-interest is driving leadership, then although it may help a leader survive the day, month, or year, it eventually is ineffective for all stakeholders. Self-interest feeds only one's ego, and followers know when leaders act only to cover for themselves while leaving everyone else out. If love isn't part of how you lead, hatred might have crept in to replace it.

I have not a met a school leader who actively leads with hatred, but I have experienced many for whom love is not in the equation. Dr. Martin Luther King Jr. said, "I have decided to stick with love because hate is a burden too heavy to bear,"[3] even though he bore the brunt of hatred through threats, violence, and the injustice to which he was subjected, even while he moved in peace throughout the Civil Rights era.

I have never had to demand my own civil rights, so I can't speak to how Dr. King led a life of passion through peace. As a leader, I have tried to choose love, not just over hatred but also over indifference, bureaucracy, bias, or my own ego. None of these feelings can be labeled as hate, and none are meant to hurt those you lead, but they do.

Here are some examples of the absence of love:

- When a staff member asks for help and a leader ignores the person
- When a leader makes a decision based on political expedience instead of investing time to understand an issue more fully
- When a leader points to policy instead of being creative in tackling a unique challenge that calls for more than a consultation of the manual

All these instances may not be driven by hate, but they will build resentment in followers. When stakeholders feel they don't matter, they are far more likely to act out on the emotions that come with the perceptions that a leader is not acting on behalf of his or her followers. This is why stakeholders can have such visceral reactions, and, when asked about their leadership, can respond by saying, "I hate them!"

How Love Affects the "Heart" of Leaders

It hasn't always been easy to lead with love, and I've certainly failed along the way, because making decisions that affect many also ultimately affected me. The unique role of school leaders, especially those in public-facing positions such as principal or superintendent, are far more vulnerable to criticism and negative reactions to their decisions. Leaders who work with direct reports, students, and families daily are open to great public pressure and often calculate decisions based on what's safe for them versus what's best for culture and community.

This is not to slight department heads or other people who don't interact as much publicly, but being visible to your stakeholders influences the decisions you'll make on their behalf; there's the ability to receive direct feedback while leading in their presence. There is a high level of accountability and opportunity to behave with love, but also to dismiss it because of the full commitment it takes to continually act with compassion, empathy, and responsibility.

Love does not have to be a grand gesture. In fact, it's the many small gestures that compound over time and provide children and adults with feelings of love, belongingness, and support. Here are some acts of love that my students or staff members have noticed or felt:

- Seeing a child or adult who seemed upset and spending time with that person
- Being fair, firm, and consistent in my approaches, whether it was pedological, procedural, or disciplinary
- Forgiving often and holding no grudges
- Putting the needs of everyone else before myself
- Being visible, present, and available, regardless of my schedule or demands of the day
- Offering immediate attention when emergencies arose
- Reminding myself (and everyone around me) that all things can be handled with time, effort, and energy
- Revealing who I am as a person, including interests, passions, and backstory
- Having fun, even in high-pressure situations

Meet Uncle Pete

I've had the good fortune of learning from excellent leadership role models in my professional career and in my family. Pete Foss, my wife's uncle, was an especially impactful person in my life, as he was for the hundreds of men who served under him in the Army during wartime fighting in Korea and Vietnam, and the hundreds more who were his journalism students during his "retirement" as a community college professor.

A 1951 graduate of West Point, he rose to the rank of colonel before retiring and teaching at North Shore Community College in Danvers, Massachusetts. Pete's Army days were over by the time I met him after I started dating my wife in 1992. There was much to love about Pete, who was an avid storyteller, reader, and a horse player like me. I got to enjoy Peter's stories on the many four-hour drives he and I took together, traveling from Boston to Saratoga Springs, New York, to bet on the ponies at the historic Saratoga Race Course.

Pete's war stories were like none I had heard before. They were not the standard blood and guts or senseless violence as portrayed in movies. Humanity lived at the center of all of his stories and showed up in the least likely places—wartime conflict. Some of these tales were desperately sad, such as the private who died the day he became a US citizen. Others were about the sheer luck of survival, such as the time his squad walked into an ambush, and he found himself drawing a pistol almost within arm's length of an enemy officer, who drew his pistol at the same time. Miraculously, both men misfired. Pete considered himself a lucky man every day after that until the end of his life.

Another story I enjoyed hearing was about lighting a fire in the dead of winter, even though Korean troops were within shooting distance. When he ordered an officer to start a fire because his troop's hot water bottles had frozen, the officer balked. Pete said it was too cold to fight that night. Shortly after the American fire was lit, Pete looked through his binoculars and smiled to see smoke from the enemy position rise into the night.

Among the many things I learned from these stories was how much Pete loved his men, the Army, and his country, and how loved he was by his troops because he consistently acted on their behalf, kept them safe, and took time to know each one individually. Throughout his life, Pete received letters of thanks from his soldiers and announcements about marriages, births, businesses opened, divorces, and even a letter from a widow informing Pete of his former soldier's death. When people—soldiers, teachers, and others—feel an emotional connection to their leadership and know they are safe to be themselves in their leader's presence, fierce loyalty and commitment are born. I believe the following story illustrates this best.

Into the Pineapple Field

As a lieutenant colonel commanding a battalion in Vietnam, Pete and his troops came on an abandoned pineapple field that they were commanded to hold. It offered an ideal place to rest, because it could be easily protected, and supplies could be dropped by planes overhead.

A problem soon arose. As men walked through the fields, their legs were getting cut by the spiky pineapple crowns that were sharp enough to tear through their army trousers. In the heat and humidity of the jungle, those cuts soon became infected because the plantation was irrigated with dirty water. Left untreated, the cuts could cause fevers and other maladies. Because medicine was not available, a staff medic recommended that the best way to clear infections was for the troops to patrol the plantation in their underwear. Pete was onboard for the unconventional, but appropriate, line of treatment because it did not place anyone in harm, and it cost nothing to try.

The next day Pete's troops received an unplanned inspection from a general, who flew in by helicopter. Pete immediately tried to explain why his men were walking in their briefs instead of their pants. Every time he opened his mouth to speak, he was cut off and given all the bureaucratic, rule-based reasons why Army soldiers should never be caught without their issued pants on. Pete recalls his hand hurting from the numerous salutes he gave the general while being brow-beaten into shape. The general promised to return for another inspection, and if Pete wanted to retain his rank, all his soldiers had better be wearing their green pants.

Pete had a leadership dilemma: For his troops to stay healthy, they had to walk the plantation in underwear. If he didn't want to be disciplined further, his troops must wear their trousers. Anyone in education who reports to someone from the building level to the superintendent's office can identify a school-based chain of command similar to what Pete faced with the same uncertainty on how to proceed in a way that protects those you lead and helps you keep your job.

Pete knew he had to stay true to the men who counted on him. He also wanted to avoid getting demoted. He used what was available to accomplish both goals.

Bordering one edge of the plantation was a small mission church with a bell. Pete stationed privates at the church around the clock with only one duty: When you see the inspecting general's helicopter approaching, ring that bell and don't stop until the helicopter is about to land. The bell was the troop's signal to put on their trousers and be ready for whenever the inspecting general reappeared. In this way, the men were kept safe, the inspecting general held his authority, and Pete kept his command.

I wasn't even a leader when I first heard Pete tell me this story, but at the time I understood it as being an important leadership lesson. From my own experience and hearing my father's frustrations from more than thirty years of teaching, I knew I would face nonsensical, demeaning, and even hurtful orders from my superiors at school. Like Pete, I would have to determine the most respectful course of action for my staff members while providing the safest solution available. Someone, maybe me, would have to ring that bell, warning all of the impending danger and stopping what we were doing to meet the expectations of higher-ups who didn't always understand the circumstances at the classroom or school level and only sought fidelity.

Love and the Demands of Leadership

The essence of leadership is being faced with conflicting demands and no clear path to arrive at what's best. This is exactly why leaders who plan with love in mind are holding themselves up to a greater standard than the simple, easily followed bureaucracy of the moment. Was Pete breaking the rules? Technically, yes; morally, no. His inspecting general cared nothing for the potential harm that could come to Pete's men, and he didn't even want to hear anything other than "Yes, sir" while showing no curiosity about why the men were walking in their underwear and, thus, he couldn't empathize.

The desire for fidelity from leaders is understandable and logical. We ascend into leadership to impart our knowledge and our experience to those we lead. But if we leave our hearts out of unique circumstances that require a better response, and we don't empathetically see necessary breaks in the rules, we will find ourselves with no one to lead. Followers are looking for inspiration, someone to show them a way when the rules and hierarchy provide no straightforward answer, either within written or unwritten rules.

Pete's men loved him because he did what was necessary and right to keep them all safe and alive. This doesn't mean all his men made it home, because they didn't. It meant that he put them in the best possible position to work, live, and fight together. Hundreds of notes of thanks piled up long after he retired because there was something memorable about how he led. Even in life-and-death situations, he showed his troops how much he loved and cared for them.

Taking the steps to love staff members for their strengths and their weaknesses allows them to love you for yours in return. The challenge is taking the steps to use love in how you lead, and this requires vulnerability—an openness to try, to share your struggles, and ultimately to open the way for staff members to lend support and suggestions to you when you struggle. And if you're wondering how to put vulnerability into practice as a leader, we will explore it in chapter 4.

Reflections on How Life Should Be

- Our jobs are callings that require us to love what we do and to lead with love.
- Educators such as Toney Jackson and Kent Brewer, who had strong foundations of love already established in their classrooms and schools, made a more effective transition to post-COVID distance learning.
- Model love by reaching out to connect with colleagues, too, even if it's just as simple as starting a book club.
- A true leader finds a way to satisfy higher-ups while serving "the troops," as exemplified in the story of Uncle Pete and the pineapple farm.
- Leadership means being faced with conflicting demands, but success will come when you rely on love to serve stakeholders and their interests.

Vulnerability

The moment leaders leave the room, everyone is free to start talking about them. And, quite often, they do. A fellow principal, Jeff Dees, taught me this hard fact some time ago, and it's always stayed with me. Once you realize that followers always will have opinions about their leaders, and that they'll often want to share those opinions, you'll have to decide how you deal with the vulnerability that's an inherent part of leadership.

Vulnerability is not just part of being a leader; it's part of being human. For growth-minded leaders, it's an element of the heart that can be used with great success by the head. In my case, instead of blaming my staff members for daring to discuss anything about me, I learned to let awareness of what was going on behind the scenes inform my thinking. I often asked myself, "What would I like those I lead to say about me in my absence?"

Vulnerability is a key part of bringing your whole self to the leadership experience and becoming an authentic leader of the head and heart. Similar to much of what I present for you to read and consider here, it can be challenging to accept the idea of admitting your own vulnerability in a work setting. But if the goal of schools is to develop learners' growth (and everyone under your leadership is a learner), the leader has to learn and grow as well. Everyone in school needs to know that perfection is not only impossible but also it is not the goal. Aim instead to use your whole vulnerable heart in all that you do to model and elicit growth in your followers.

Perfectly Imperfect Leadership

Through eleven years of leading schools in four districts, I have had the opportunity to work with about seventy principals, and there were just a handful who were so engaging, committed, and open enough that I would have gladly worked with them again. Jeff Dees is one of those people.

Jeff stuck out just a little bit in Wellesley, Massachusetts, where we worked together. He grew up in Dallas, Texas, and Little Rock, Arkansas, and he spoke in a twangy drawl, not the quick, clipped accent of Bay State natives. But to mistake this difference in speech as a lack of intelligence, as some did, was to miss Jeff's brilliance in school leadership. (Still, it happened. A parent once left a series of expletive-filled notes on his car windshield encouraging him to go back to wherever he was from.)

Jeff's passion and pragmatism were enough for me to sit up straighter and listen any time he contributed at leadership meetings. He didn't mince words or tee up difficult subjects up with niceties. He's a "let's get to the point and figure this out together" kind of leader. He knows what he knows and, just as important, he knows what *he doesn't know*. He's not afraid to be vulnerable, and he modeled for me what a true asset that can be. In fact, many of our conversations have begun with one of us saying, "I have a challenge, and I'm not sure what to do here. Can you help me?"

The Strength to Admit Vulnerability

To trust a leadership colleague enough to admit a shortcoming requires tremendous vulnerability. Leaders often act like middle school students: so concerned about their status and self-worth that they find it difficult to unmask what they don't know or even admit to making a mistake. When Jeff and I were colleagues, we worked with a leader who was so hyper-focused on his own perception of strength that he failed to support his team, especially when a dilemma arose in school. This leader could not admit he didn't know something or didn't have ready answers. He was operating from a fixed mindset by believing that leaders need to be perfect and that they aren't in need of the same professional learning that we expect our teachers to receive.

Jeff knew his own stakeholders would discuss his words and actions the moment he stepped away from a meeting. Unlike our boss, he also knew that he could better serve everyone by being authentic and vulnerable with whomever he was meeting, because he couldn't possibly have all the answers. Instead of hiding what he didn't know or where he may need help, Jeff exposed his challenges and willingly asked for help. His followers appreciated the opportunities to assist him and be on his team.

Mindset Moment

I learned a lesson about my own resistance to vulnerability during a multi-year investigation into growth mindset research with the staff at the Fiske School. It happened after I provided my staff members with a growth mindset survey, which followed two years of training for all stakeholders. We had done so much good work together that I was anticipating an average score in the nineties on a hundred-point scale.

Imagine my surprise and discomfort when I tabulated all forty respondents and came away with an average score of seventy-eight. I was so angry that it took me two school days and a weekend to calm down, reflect on the results, and determine a course of action. My initial reaction was to fight what I perceived as low results, reflecting my staff members' problem. My mindset was fixed, but eventually I saw the results as the opportunity to find a better way forward. The results made clear that I had to improve opportunities for shared leadership, which took time for me to realize.

If love is a law to obey, vulnerability is the compass that leads us there. Remember, just the act of saying "I love you" or behaving in ways that show love was difficult for Kent Brewer to do—at first. Kent is the kind, low-key elementary school leader from chapter 3. He actually hemmed and hawed deciding if he should even say "I love you" at school. Why? Likely due to self-preservation—most of us either haven't leveraged love or are only considering how to be more intentional with love at school. He didn't want to be seen as different. His initial fear of vulnerability got in the way of being more generous with love at school, but he learned to overcome such misgivings with encouragement.

Value in Vulnerability

Our work in education is not for the faint of heart, but it is vital in setting a course of collaboration and cultivation that ultimately enables a leader to curate what's important at the individual and collective levels in classes, departments, and districts. My first year as the MacArthur Elementary School principal, I broke the cardinal rule for any first-year leader: I took on a potential large-scale change before fully understanding the school culture.

Every first-year leader will immediately pick up cultural elements that don't match their values or those that are stated by the school or district. It can be difficult to ignore or put off procedure, policy, and pedagogy that grates against your perception of what's right. The consequence for acting with a "ready, jump, set" mentality is that you are likely to miss important histories or the emotional and political fallout that occurs when leaders move too quickly and aren't quite known, or trusted, by their staff members.

Change Makes Everyone Vulnerable

Any time school leadership makes changes, they are putting educators in vulnerable positions of not knowing what to do, how to do it, and whom to ask for help. Schools also can be guilty of making decisions quickly without considering the consequences or even preparing for them, as found in these examples:

- Curriculum adoptions delivered without teacher feedback or planned professional development
- Technology purchases made without consideration for stated goals, software, pedagogy, and time for practice
- Strategic plan rewrites based solely on leadership goals instead of student outcomes
- Addressing complex challenges such as equity, inclusion, or bias with simplistic, one-time presentations

Any of these leadership moves has the ability to disrupt teacher equilibrium, and being knocked off balance can be disruptive and instructive: disruptive because no one wants to teach through uncertainty, instructive because teaching and learning are always in a constant state of flux. Yes, there are tried-and-true methods that lead to successful outcomes. Some of those methods should already be undergoing change based on research, technology, and our constant reexamination of how our brains most effectively learn. For instance, if we are teaching solely for knowledge attainment that students can gather through a basic internet search, we are not harnessing all that technology can do to elevate learning to higher standards and competencies.

When I crossed the river from Boston into Cambridge to continue teaching fifth grade, I encountered a colleague who voiced his frustration at professional development by asking, "Why do we have to keep learning new things? Can't we just be allowed to teach?" There's certainly enough poorly planned and executed professional development to go around, so my colleague's sentiment has likely been echoed in your school district, too. Understandable, yes; acceptable, not quite.

My mentor and former middle school principal and superintendent, John D'Auria, told me, "You're not going to have student growth without educator growth." Almost everything school leaders do, regardless of where they lead, must be connected to the growth of adults, so ultimately more students will learn and grow.

A leader doesn't have to do everything in the first, second, or third year on the job. With leadership maturity, focusing on culture, and acting with love, leaders can better marshal resources for what's important, especially when it requires a school- or district-wide change. So much change already is foisted on educators by federal, state, or even local boards or departments. Local leaders are wise to be careful in how they set up conditions for change.

The Weakness of "My Way or the Highway"

Being an open, vulnerable leader lies in direct opposition to the leadership model we see portrayed in the movies. There, a leader takes command, gives decisive orders that are unilaterally followed, and obtains universal respect. Who wouldn't like to ride horseback in front of battle-ready troops like Mel Gibson's William Wallace character in *Braveheart*? Or maybe you'd rather be like that lightning-rod principal Joe Clark, as played by Morgan Freeman in the movie *Lean on Me*. Clark was a "my way or the highway" disciplinarian who immediately expelled more than three hundred students in an effort to regain order at a struggling high school in Paterson, New Jersey.

> ### Today and Tomorrow
>
> **Today.** Be aware that you can't be a perfect leader so find ways to present your authentic self. At your next staff meeting, share a story about a time something was hard to learn, but you learned it, and share a story about something you gave up on and wished you hadn't. Ask your staff members to share their stories, too.
>
>
>
> **Tomorrow.** An openness to vulnerability takes a growth mindset approach. Normalize mistake-making in classrooms, departments, and schools by sharing your struggles within a well-understood and shared framework such as Critical Friends, which provides structures and supports for having difficult conversations that help educators listen intently and work toward solutions together. Frame meetings and evaluations on what can be learned and how it can be learned, and emphasize process over product.

Here in the real world, it's not long before decisiveness can become divisive if it occurs without input or feedback from followers. Leading with the head and heart requires something more, such as asking these reflective questions: "Why am I doing this?" "Whom does this benefit?" "Whom can I ask for help?" "Does this align with our values?"

Sometimes a warrior is needed, either on the battlefield or in the conference room. But a warrior is not what's required in every situation. Leaders simply can't always take the helm alone to be effective in the long term. Beyond the reflective questions, leaders need staff members to test, probe, and challenge their thinking. A head and heart leader knows that one person simply can't foresee all current obstacles or future challenges without the help of the greater community of people who hold expertise and have experiences that can help inform decisions for the greater good.

Vulnerability During (Inevitable) Mistakes

I wasn't actively taking up a charge to lead when I suggested my school join another in an expanded learning time grant the Massachusetts Department of Education was offering. By school year's end I certainly felt like the cavalry was headed my way. It seemed simple in the beginning. Another Waltham principal sent an email asking for volunteers to take part in the grant. The state required two schools per district to sign onto a two-year self-study. If the grant were successful, both schools would extend their school day by ninety minutes. I really should have known better than to jump into this. It was a major undertaking that required the two schools to do a lot of work:

- Form an exploratory team composed of parents and staff.
- Survey staff members and families about extending the school day.
- Participate in statewide meetings.
- Study the impact of a longer school day in year one and conduct a school-wide staff vote on it in year two, with a two-thirds majority required to be in favor of extension.
- For the school to qualify, the school district had to open school choice to the entire school district, allowing students to opt in or out.

If the first four bullets weren't concerning enough, the final one should have opened my eyes. Waltham was a school district with six elementary schools based on geography, meaning that children who lived within the confines of a school population zone attended one of six schools. Opening up school choice within the district because of a state grant awarded to just two schools would throw school populations, staffing, and transportation into disarray. I didn't learn this until pretty late in first year of the study, and I almost paid dearly for it.

The study itself started off well. We gathered a diverse team of staff members and families, saw generally positive interest through surveys sent out to every family, and attended off-site state events to learn more. The team and our school stakeholders were encouraged to voice their opinions. As year one started to wind down, I started hearing strong arguments for and against extending our learning day.

The work we were doing gained the attention of the town's mayor, who was also the head of the school committee. A very strong mayor, she had instituted quarterly, citywide school-parent meetings, which every principal was required to attend. Building leaders could be questioned at any time, without preparation and often not understanding the parental or mayoral issue being discussed. It was not a pleasant meeting to attend at the best of times.

When word reached the mayor about how school choice might affect all schools, my expanded learning time principal colleague and I were called to a special meeting of parents to explain the grant and it's not-so-positive implications for the entire district. Instead of nine principals on call, there would only be two. (Actually, it came down to a meeting of one, when my colleague called out sick that day.)

Meanwhile, within my school, concerns were voiced when I was in the teacher's room, walking the hallways, or even out at recess. One camp was strongly in favor of winning the grant and one was just as vehemently against it. And if I was hearing these remarks as I traveled through the building, I could only imagine what was being said when I left those rooms.

Opening the Door to Vulnerability

Between the mayor's displeasure and my staff members now beginning to argue with each other and me, I realized I had made a dreadful mistake joining the grant. I had exposed the vulnerabilities of my staff, and the culture we were trying to curate together was in jeopardy. Our culture was not yet mature enough to handle the high stakes that expanded learning time would place on us, especially if anything less than an overwhelming majority of staff members agreed. I had needlessly put my own reputation on the line within the first nine months on the job. I was going to have to open the door to my own vulnerability to salvage my school and, potentially, my job.

Although the state-mandated school team formation, statewide meetings, and surveys had been helpful, they had not exposed all the fears and anxieties that were now coming to the forefront. I knew I had to take action that went outside the parameters of the grant if I were to maintain the positive culture I had begun curating. I needed to make sure the staff members exited this debacle with dignity and a feeling of belonging, no matter which side of the issue they were on.

I called a state representative who was serving as our mentor and told him I had made the decision to ask for a staff vote at the end of the first year, instead of the second, due to the raw emotion and volatility I was sensing. I added that instead of the state-mandated two-thirds staff vote in favor, I was going to require a three-fourths majority to continue. He urged me to wait, continue the study, and vote next school year. I kindly said I knew what I had done, and I knew I had to act now.

I unwittingly exposed previously unknown vulnerabilities in my school and my district. My ignorance was uncovered, and it was important for me to share the experience with my staff members during a special faculty meeting where we would vote for or against moving forward with year two of the grant. I carefully explained that I wasn't for or against the grant moving forward, that I had made a mistake taking this on, and that I would live by my mandate of a three-quarters vote no matter where it took us. One staff member asked to debate the issue at hand, and I denied her request, telling her debate had been going on long enough. Further discussion would only escalate the situation.

Was I decisive? Sure. Did it take courage to buck the state rules? Absolutely. Were my goals in calling for an early vote set forth with empathy for my staff members and self-preservation? Yes and yes. I knew that if I wanted to continue to lead at MacArthur, I needed an exit strategy for my staff members and me. I took the vote before the scheduled citywide parent-mayor meeting so I would be prepared with an explanation. I was willing to be vulnerable with my staff members and the mayor, with the goal of learning from the experience and moving forward with greater inclusivity and dignity.

I counted the votes back at my office. The results were just one vote short of a three-fourths majority in favor. True to my word, I shared the results and my thoughts with the staff through a long email. I explained my process and the mistakes I had learned from it; I thanked the expanded learning time team and offered my apologies for putting so many people in a difficult position during my first year. I wanted all to know this was a challenge I had created, and if they were upset with the results, I invited them to share their displeasure with me. Only one staff member came to see me, and I'll share her reaction in chapter 5.

Vulnerability and the Myth of Perfection

My first full-time gig was as a city hall reporter for a small daily newspaper responsible for writing two stories a day from 5 am to 10 am. It was a stressful job that was made worse by the fact that I'm a horrible speller.

During my first three months on the job, I would submit my two stories and then go to the bathroom to throw up. I was terrified of making mistakes that all our readers might see. As it happened, I made plenty of them, including spelling errors that managed to slip by my editors. After three months, I had a thicker skin, and I'd also dedicated myself to becoming better by learning from my mistakes so as not to repeat them.

My editors and our readers let me know what I was doing wrong, but your staff members may not be as forthcoming, especially if you aren't modeling vulnerability. If a leader can't be viewed as human, it can lead to greater difficulties down the road when stakeholders fear coming to you with the challenges that will inevitably arise.

Vulnerability ultimately becomes more freeing than the mythological bonds that come with being an all-knowing leader. When leaders open themselves to modeling the complete process of learning, from failure through to success, they set the tone for what they expect. Dr. Carol Dweck, growth mindset researcher and author of *Mindset*, says employers shouldn't expect employees to be perfect, but instead she stresses we're all works in process.[1]

I have worked with and coached leaders struggling with vulnerability, including veterans and those new to the endeavor. The fallacy that a leader can get everything right is seen by most stakeholders as fiction—a leader who is not accessible and available to followers is not real.

Taking Thirty Seconds: Annette Addair

Annette Addair walks through the Chandler, Arizona, elementary school she leads with the intensity of a principal on a mission. She leads a staff that serves children who live in abject poverty, where it's not uncommon for students to have to walk under or around crime scene tape on their way to school. Her short, quick strides are purposeful because they have to be.

Her wall-length office whiteboard is filled with some eighty-plus tasks and initiatives the Galveston Elementary is currently undertaking. Her "A Team" leadership group sits and assesses the status of what's been undertaken and what's most urgent or possible in the coming weeks. There is no downtime.

Helping children to thrive through varied circumstances of poverty is a lot to consider, experience, and manage for the Galveston staff, as it is for schools serving the approximately twenty-eight million poor children in America.[2] Addair's fierce belief in all children and developing the means to help them is evident in everything she does. She carries all the emotions, curriculum, pedagogy, assessment, and so on wherever she goes through twelve-hour workdays that start before anyone arrives and end long after staff members go home. That kind of strain can be hard on a leader's head and heart.

Part of my coaching with Addair was to help her consider how working so hard against such difficult circumstances affects her and her staff members. I nudged her and suggested that if she were able to model her own vulnerability more often it would help her staff members understand the human toll such important work can take. Meeting the emotional needs of everyone at school had to include opportunities for Addair to share her struggles. Not long after our discussion an opportunity for vulnerability presented itself.

Right before a faculty meeting, Addair was assisting with a challenging student who had made a habit of bolting from school, often. On this day, the finding, chasing, and ensuring the child's safety was especially trying. There were only a few moments for Addair to reapply her trademark bright lipstick and transition from a student experience that had left her shaken to leading a meeting. As she tried to start the meeting, she just couldn't. Her eyes welled up, her voice quivered, and she paused, telling her staff members, "I'm sorry; I need thirty seconds before I begin." Everyone waited quietly while she composed herself. Reflecting on this moment, Addair said, "It was the longest and best thirty seconds."

Similar to many school leaders, Addair had assumed she had been vulnerable with her staff members by asking for help and showing she wasn't all-knowing, but that wasn't enough. In actually witnessing her stop and compose herself before carrying on with the work of leading, Addair was sharing herself with her teachers—modeling that it was okay to acknowledge emotions that can surface—and demonstrating that they can't always be controlled.

"The teachers recognized my vulnerability before I did," she says. "It was a confirmation for me and them. They didn't roll their eyes. They responded with grace."

Addair's vulnerable moment wasn't a planned agenda item. I may have planted the seeds for her to consider a more vulnerable side of leadership, but she took the moment when it arose, simply hoping it was the right thing to do. From those thirty seconds, Addair felt that her staff members had her back and she could more fully have theirs.

Leaders not embracing vulnerability are telling those they lead that perfection, even though misguided, is what they must embrace. This means that obstacles, challenges, and mistakes that occur daily are not up for discussion, that leaders will not take on a chink in their leadership armor to help or assist. The consistent message from this kind of infallible leader is, "You figure it out and keep the problem from reaching or affecting me."

Psychological Safety

How you recognize and become more vulnerable is to embrace your mistakes and present them to whole groups of colleagues or those you lead as learning experiences, not only for yourself but for all. Amy Edmondson's work on psychological safety is worth exploring, because she sees mistakes as the beginning of a solution, not a sign of the absence of leadership. Edmondson, a Harvard professor, has published research on psychological safety since 1999; has written a book, *The Fearless Organization;* and can be seen on a TEDx Talk, "Building a Psychologically Safe Workplace."

Edmondson defines psychological safety as "a shared belief held by members of a team that the team is safe for interpersonal risk taking." In one study, Edmondson and her research teams studied how hospitals dealt with prescribed medication mistakes. She ranked hospitals by their mistakes per one thousand drugs given and found that hospitals ranged from making seven to twenty-five mistakes. Her researchers then studied teams at each hospital to understand how those teams understood, learned from, and remediated mistakes.[3]

Common sense would dictate that the highest-performing hospitals would have the fewest number of mistakes. In fact, researchers found just the opposite. It was the hospitals with *more* mistakes that were higher functioning. They were constantly working on improving practices and outcomes. That's because staff members at the high-performing hospitals felt confident in reporting mistakes to their peers and superiors, and mistakes were openly discussed during rounds and meetings. Because the culture focused on improvement, the attitude was that mistakes were crucial to the learning process.

The hospitals reporting fewer mistakes actually were making just as many mistakes as the higher reporting teams, but they weren't confident in sharing them, due to a lack of psychological safety. In this group, mistakes were viewed as the equivalent of red marks on a student's homework. They were never discussed, because improvement wasn't the goal. Within a team that has no tolerance for mistakes, the fear of exposing failure overrides the importance of discussing the mistake and learning how to improve. You can't avoid mistakes if you can't discuss the processes, procedures, and decision-making that went into making them. Edmondson suggests three ways leaders can ensure the kind of psychological safety that can create high-performing teams:

- Acknowledge your own infallibility.
- Frame challenges as learning problems for the department, not as execution problems by an individual.
- Model curiosity and ask lots of questions.

The Problem with "Problems of Practice"

I've experienced firsthand how challenging it can be for some leaders to adopt those three simple principles Edmondson suggests. My superintendent in Wellesley began to hold "problems of practice" presented by school building leaders at our biweekly leadership meetings. I give him props for attempting to normalize mistakes, indecision, and not knowing what to do. The idea was to share our problems and see if our leadership colleagues could offer feedback and suggestions for improved outcomes.

Unfortunately, we stopped presenting our problems of practice after only a few tries.

Although the rationale behind the turnaround wasn't shared with us on the leadership team, I wouldn't be surprised to learn "problems of practice" was scrapped from our agenda because the superintendent didn't have all the answers to the multitude of challenges building leaders were willing to share.

Edmondson describes four zones of feelings depending on how your levels of psychological safety and accountability intersect. Many leaders feel they are in positions of high accountability—based on test scores, improving graduation rates, working with multiple stakeholders simultaneously, and so on—and low psychological safety. Edmondson calls this the "anxiety zone." The ideal is have both high accountability and high psychological safety, which Edmondson calls the "learning zone." For more on the four zones please see her TEDx Talk mentioned previously in the chapter.

From the Anxiety Zone to the Learning Zone

All of Edmondson's suggestions came into play when I first started asking questions of my staff members. I wanted to know what they needed from me, how they wanted to improve, and what might be getting in the way. Asking questions humanizes leaders and shows that we're vulnerable enough to admit that we need information and feedback from our stakeholders in order to lead well. It is the ultimate sharing of what's inside a leader's heart.

During my first full day of professional development, I asked all my teachers at MacArthur a simple question: "What support do you need?" Overwhelmingly, they told me they needed help teaching writers' workshop. I then asked follow-up questions. "When was the writing initiative started? How had you been supported before my arrival? What parts of writers' workshop delivery do you need the most help with?"

What I learned was that writers' workshop—an incredibly intentional and detailed format for teaching writing—was shared with all elementary teachers the year before my arrival as part of a back-to-school training. Staff members told me they were presented with five overhead slides in fifteen minutes and were expected to then deliver this complex methodology without any further training. The result was the delivery of uneven and uncertain writing instruction. At the same time, there was a high expectation of accountability from the director of elementary literacy. It was what Edmondson refers to as the anxiety zone—high accountability with low psychological safety.

If staff members were caught not "performing" writers' workshop with a few stated elements, they were in trouble for not teaching with fidelity. Because I asked, I found out that none of my teachers felt comfortable delivering effective writers' workshop instruction. So, the problem was a learning problem, in which staff members needed greater support, and not an execution problem, in which they just weren't doing what they were told. In fact, they had no idea how to even get started.

Although I had some writing experience, I was not the person to best help my teachers. I knew I had to reach out and find a writers' workshop expert. I acknowledged to my staff members that we could learn this, I was invested, but I needed to find someone to provide hours of professional development for all teachers so we could learn and grow in a safe and supportive environment. Edmondson would categorize this as the learning zone—high accountability with high psychological safety.

The Promise of Vulnerability

To be vulnerable is to be human, and every day there are thousands of interactions at school in which mistakes or misunderstandings can occur. That's why it's so important that educational leaders model how to live with their vulnerability. Leaders can norm the processes of learning and growing, including the inevitability of making mistakes, asking for help, and seeking feedback at frequent intervals.

Requesting help from those you're supposed to lead can be new for many, but leaders' failure to embrace their vulnerability detracts from their leadership for the purpose of propping up a fragile ego. It's as if their heads do not want to allow their hearts equal leadership footing. The cost of posing as the all-knowing leader who has to be right, or at least perceived as being right, is sure to build resentment in stakeholders whom leaders are supposed to engage and inspire. That resentment can create a greater number of stakeholders who are willing to fight or sabotage a leader's mission.

By opening yourself to vulnerability, you'll be establishing a larger pattern of servitude as part of your leadership style. In chapter 5, I outline how to engage your heart empathetically with stakeholders and behave with their dignity in mind. These two key elements of servant leadership enable leaders to appreciate each person uniquely and focus on improving the process, not the person, so that all can fulfill their role to their highest potential.

Reflections on How Life Should Be

- The moment a leader leaves a room, everyone in the room is free to talk about that person. Instead of blaming my staff members for daring to discuss anything about me, I learned to let awareness of what was going on behind the scenes inform my thinking. I often asked myself, "What would I like those I lead to say about me in my absence?"
- If the goal of schools is to develop learners and growth, the leader has to learn and grow as well. Making mistakes, and learning from them, creates a growth mindset culture.

- Implementing change—a fact of life in education—makes everyone more vulnerable, so do it mindfully.
- Amy Edmondson's research on psychological safety in the workplace shows high-performing teams acknowledge their own fallibility; frame challenges as learning problems for the department, not as execution problems by an individual; and model curiosity by asking lots of questions.
- If a leader can't be viewed as human, it can lead to greater difficulties down the road when stakeholders fear coming to you with the challenges that will inevitably arise.

5

Empathy + Dignity

ometimes leaders get hugs and "I love yous." Sometimes we get nothing but criticism. As a head and heart leader, you'll come to realize that servant leadership can get you through every encounter, whether positive or painful, because a leader must be willing to give without any guarantee of what will be offered in return.

Here's an example of how easily our expectations can be sidetracked and how behaving with an in-service-first approach can help you get back on track. On the first day of school one year, a kindergartener was returned to our school at the end of the day by her bus driver. From the driver it was unclear if the parent or a relative wasn't at the stop, the child missed her stop, or if the student was even on the right bus. Complicating matters the child spoke only Russian because her mother had moved to Waltham to attend a nearby university.

I welcomed the child back to school, called the parent, then sat with the girl for forty-five minutes until her mother arrived. It was a challenging situation not being able communicate and console a student. She was tearful and confused about why she'd been returned to school, and all I could do was offer a comforting heart presence, serving my student by staying at her side. Then her mother arrived, and I got a leadership challenge I had not expected.

I had anticipated meeting a grateful parent who would eagerly listen to my explanation of school policy about what happens when kindergarteners don't get off at their correct stop. I even expected to receive a warm "thank you for sitting and waiting with my daughter." But the girl's mother had nothing but angry questions about how this could possibly have happened. I tried to explain again, only to be met with more consternation. Before I decided to go forward with a third try, I checked my heart and observed the situation more closely. Reading the parent's face and hearing her escalating voice, I tried this instead: "Obviously, I am not giving you what you need. So, what do you need?"

Her reply was straightforward: "I want someone to take responsibility." "Oh," I said. "That's easy. Since I'm the principal, I'm responsible. It's my fault. I will make sure it never happens again."

Giving Up on Being Right

Top secret principal tip: There were no actions I had personally taken that led to a kindergartener missing her bus stop after the first day of school. But, on another level, I knew that it was, in fact, my fault. I was in charge of everything at the school. When I told the upset mother I'd make sure it would never happen again, I didn't even know what the "it" was. I did know that I was going to find out. I planned that my first duty the next day would be to check in with the kindergarten teacher responsible for getting the child on the bus. I knew I would treat that teacher with the same empathy and dignity I had afforded the mother and daughter.

In leading with head and heart, you'll come to understand that being right is overrated. I knew the kindergarten team had worked together on a process to get our littlest students on the right bus on day one of school. But, if something had gone awry in the walk from the class to the bus, it was my job to figure that out and work with the teachers to prevent another incident. In meeting with the student's teacher first thing the next morning, we concluded that the child may have simply followed a new friend onto the wrong bus. Our remedy: The teacher would escort the student to her bus each day until she could do so more independently at dismissal.

Learning from Lucille

From inheriting problems that were not my doing to consequences of my own accord, there were always situations to learn from and grow. As I explained in chapter 4, I had created a problem in my school by applying for a grant when I was ignorant of the intended and unintended consequences of expanding the learning day. I knew it was my duty to explain myself to my staff members, so I carefully communicated a message of resolution via email following our school's decision to exit the expanded learning time grant, and I included an invitation to see me if further questions or concerns arose. Veteran first-grade teacher Lucille Horgan was the only teacher to take me up on the offer.

Like me, Lucille was one of MacArthur's earliest arrivals each school day. After thirty years of teaching, she still came to school with high levels of commitment, energy, and enthusiasm for her job. When Lucille came to see me that morning after the school's vote, she stood at the door and said, "Anthony, you did good. You allowed everyone to escape with their dignity and move on."

As a new leader to the building, this was the stamp of validation I needed. If Lucille was feeling this way, I knew I had snatched some small victory through this very difficult learning experience. As I have continued to reflect on that moment of potential fallout, I am reminded that my intention was to correct my wrongs by thinking of my staff members first and hoping I made the right moves to better inform our culture moving forward.

What I received in return was empathy and dignity, not just from Lucille but also from the entire staff. The gift of reconciliation I provided to my staff members was returned to me tenfold in the expressions of thanks that followed Lucille's. I was less worried about being right and more concerned with actions that could build a bridge back to an inclusive school culture—service first, ego in check.

What We Do for the Least of Us

Whenever a leader is faced with anger or an escalation, it's easy to turn toward self-preservation by proving that you're right. Whether the leader is right or not is of little consequence when a teacher is crying, a child has flipped a table, or a board member is demanding a favor for a constituent. Chief among the many responsibilities for a leader is to figure out the needs of stakeholders and fill those needs in dignified ways that enable a leader to ensure the self-worth of whomever they are charged with helping. Leaders have to face themselves and their decisions continually; contemplating what they've done within their values and vision reinforces behaviors based on serving.

Sometimes adults and children alike just need a face-saving after their vulnerability has been exposed for all to see. Vulnerability can show up as a ten-year-old spending twenty minutes calling you every name in the book, a veteran staff member protesting during a faculty meeting, or a parent demanding accountability. Quietly waiting on the ten-year-old until he has used every expletive, responding to the staff member with a curious question, or asking the parent what she wants are dignified responses because they recognize the situations are fraught with potential landmines of trouble. With the end result in mind to soothe, understand, or find middle ground, a leader who listens with empathy worries less about status and more about serving.

Mindset Moment

My fifth grader, Adam, had been acting out and receiving consequences from me all week. I was tired and so was he. That day's writing prompt was "What is your most prized possession?" Adam wrote, "My most prized possession is my pillow, because my mom is being treated for cancer, and I have to stay at different friends' and family member's houses each night. My pillow is the only thing that reminds me of home and my mom."

Gulp! Instead of empathizing with Adam, I had treated his behavior as disruptive, without wondering what might be going on in his life. From that day forward I greeted Adam by saying, "Thank you for coming to school today." I also learned to always ask my students, "Has anything changed at home or school lately?" when they showed sudden changes in behavior.

In the course of my career, I've often responded to traumatized children acting on fight, flight, or freeze responses hardwired into their heads and hearts from harmful experiences. This included a fair share of locating and returning children who had run from class or school. Support staff members and I could take anywhere from five minutes to three hours during these responses because we were at the mercy of trying to shift a child's lifelong experiences with behaviors based on neurological responses developed for self-preservation.

After one lengthy but successful response of returning a student to school who had run outside to the playground, a teacher asked me, "How do you even know do what to do?" I just shrugged and said, "Not sure, but I just do." The real answer includes these resources:

- Tapping reserves of patience I didn't know I had
- Understanding it's not about you, but the child you must help

- Knowing the student, including likes and interests, and wanting to know more, even during a crisis
- Using tried-and-true crisis prevention techniques, learning new ones, and simplifying adult responses for improved outcomes

Servant leadership is similar to vulnerability in that it can carry negative connotations. Yet religious texts, tribal proverbs, and ancient fables all describe the importance of serving regardless of our size or standing. Think of the mouse pulling a thorn from a lion's paw or the promise that those with the least will inherit the kingdom of heaven. When leaders empathize with others, they are taking on the feelings of those they are serving, viewing outcomes from their followers' varied perspectives, and validating where stakeholders currently stand.

An African proverb states, "The child who is not embraced by the village will burn it down to feel its warmth." This is true not only of our students but adults as well. From support staff members to school board members, I have witnessed those who don't feel seen attempt to assert themselves in all kinds of disruptive and destructive ways. Of course, schools are the village in all that we do and how we serve students, either directly at the school level or indirectly through policy, budget, food services, and curriculum decisions. Each adult has the power to act on behalf of students or *not,* with consequences.

I always told school staff members "What we do for the least of us, we do for all of us" to inspire empathy and dignity. Everyone in the school building sees what happens when we stop, notice, and care for those who have less, whether socially, cognitively, economically, physically, or emotionally. Children and adults notice when someone acting out is receiving care in the face of adversity. This reassures everyone from preschoolers to thirty-year teachers because they all can see themselves in the person being helped and they think, "If I'm ever in trouble, I will have someone who will help me." Everyone needs support at points in a school day, year, or career, including leaders.

Servant Leader in Action: Terry Roller

The chief administrative officer for the Alabama State Department of Education, Terry Roller, is responsible for helping struggling school districts transform into productive places of learning. He can "talk the talk" of school leadership because he's "walked the walk" in his twenty-seven-year career in education. Roller is known for being a sharp dresser, from his suits and bow ties to his immaculately polished shoes. He's a man with a big smile, a big heart, and a big influence on the students in his state.

Throughout his career, he's led in service to others as his guiding force for good. His goal has been to positively affect the lives of the young people he serves, and he estimates that he's directly or indirectly had a say in improving schools for about fifty thousand kids.

"Whatever the kids have needed, I've made sure they've had it," he said. This has included everything from the latest technology to baloney sandwiches. During our conversations for this book, he was taking breaks to pack and mail safety supplies to a school.

"Some may say that packing supplies is 'below my pay grade,'" he said. "As a servant leader who acts with humility and empathy, it's always my job to find and provide whatever children and adults need to become successful."

Roller knows it's important that his students experience the dignity of feeling seen. Yet when he was a young man, Roller the student felt invisible. In school, he was often argumentative with teachers, especially in math class. He purposely started arguments so he could get thrown out of class and not expose his lack of understanding. "No one cared, so I just quit trying," he said.

That changed when one adult at school took a moment to acknowledge him. Jim Richards was a history teacher and basketball coach, and he told Roller something important: "Terry, there is something about you. You are going to do great things. You are going to change lives." In the moment, Roller said he stood up two inches taller. As an adult, thirty-six years later, he still tries to live up to those words. And Richards, who became Terry's godfather, is now his nine-year-old son's godfather. Similar to Nancy Leverich, my English teacher described in chapter 3, Richards set Roller on a path of success by simply noticing something in the young man that he didn't see himself.

Whether leaders are supporting, teaching, or leading, Roller identified four critical steps for success:

- Seeing who is in front of us, whether students or staff members
- Connecting with someone by knowing his or her interest, hobby, or passion

- Valuing that person
- Giving that person a voice to speak or participate

Even as a new teacher, Roller took simple steps to ensure he could positively affect his students, all 180 of them. He created index cards for each student with his or her name, preferred nickname, interests, challenges, and phone number. He reviewed the cards and supported his students' interests, whether that meant a kind word, discussing their favorite genre of music, or buying something that showed his students he cared. "If I saw a poorly dressed student who had immaculate sneakers, I'd buy that student cleaning products to help keep those sneakers flawlessly clean," he says.

Roller also used those index cards to call all his students' homes to personally invite parents or caregivers to the school's open house. This was before cell phones, so it took weeks of calling back or leaving messages before getting confirmation for all students. When his first high school principal asked young Roller how he was able to get so many parents to school, he told her that he simply called them all to ask.

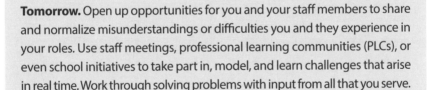

Today and Tomorrow

Today. When you're frustrated with a follower, student, or situation, try empathetically examining the other side. There may be unexplained experiences and perspectives that are in need of further understanding. Try asking either questions of curiosity or concern to reveal what you may be missing.

Tomorrow. Open up opportunities for you and your staff members to share and normalize misunderstandings or difficulties you and they experience in your roles. Use staff meetings, professional learning communities (PLCs), or even school initiatives to take part in, model, and learn challenges that arise in real time. Work through solving problems with input from all that you serve.

Leading the Way toward Belongingness

School is important in the lives of students because it's a place, separate from home, where they can belong. The challenge is that all children can feel lost, anxious, and alone in school. At Fiske School, we surveyed our students each year to better understand their levels of belongingness. This started prior to my arrival at Fiske, when the school engaged with Stan Davis, author of *Schools Where Everyone Belongs*, to meet with parents, staff members, and students to discuss, plan, and deliver on a school culture built on the intentionality of belongingness.

Our work with Davis began as an anti-bullying initiative, but it grew to embrace the goal of creating a school where we valued each individual, celebrated differences, and cared enough to problem-solve when students or staff members didn't live up to our values, instead of simply punishing them. As I wrote in chapter 2, we were devoted in defining and living our values of being **f**air, **i**nclusive, **s**afe, **k**ind, and **e**ncouraging. We knew if we attuned ourselves to these values and consistently modeled them daily, more children would feel part of the Fiske School, which would lead to happy, healthy, and successful students. Our survey included these questions:

1. Do you feel as if you belong?
2. Why do you feel this way?
3. If you have a problem, is there an adult you feel comfortable going to at school?
4. Do you understand the school rules? Are they fair?

Davis had normed these survey questions across the country and determined that when 60 percent of students or more answered "yes" to questions 1, 3, and 4, it was a sign of an effective school culture of belongingness. Fiske usually scored 80 percent or better. Students said things such as "The teachers know my name," "Teachers smile at me," "Adults at school greet us and are happy to be here." There is dignity in not only seeing your students but also in defining how you'll best work together through common values.

Roller puts it this way: "Dignity is not teaching to solve for *y*. Dignity is our *why*. It's how we make kids feel the instant they walk into our classrooms. If they feel seen just one time, they will come back 179 more times to get that one raindrop of validation."

The same can be said of our adult stakeholders of staff members and families. The mother of the returned-to-school kindergartener wanted me to actively listen with empathy and respond with dignity. At first, I was too concerned with offering explanations from my perspective to actually hear what she needed from me. Egocentrically listening only to respond or defend a leader's position usually drives interactions to frustrating ends when problems are left to linger and the situation becomes more complex and harder to solve.

The servant leadership model cares little about ego and keeping score of how followers have failed to live up to expectations or buck a leader's plans. I've always thought that when a student fails in a teacher's presence it says more about the teacher than the student. In the same way, when a school fails in a leader's presence, it is most assuredly more about the leader than the followers, for similar reasons.

Consider that teachers teach for approximately one thousand hours a school year outside breaks and duties. How often do leaders, from building principals to central office staff members, interact meaningfully with teachers during those thousand hours? Even if we agree on a high-water mark of ten hours of leadership coaching, observation, or evaluation for high-functioning schools, far too many teachers get zero. This leaves teachers learning and growing on their own for 99 percent of the time in a best-case scenario. Leadership that begins with an empathetic ear for listening and follows up with a dignified approach of support creates a reciprocal value-based relationship—a place where servant leadership blooms.

How Do They *Need* to Be Treated?

Although I present empathy + dignity as a formula, it is not like a geometric proof that you follow lockstep to solve challenges. It's more of a mindset of how to approach your followers and a model of how you'd like them to help children learn. In addition, it's not just treating others as you'd like to be treated but treating them as they *need* to be treated. Often, we treat others only from our perspective. Having worked with many children suffering from trauma, I learned to shift perspectives quickly under adverse circumstances.

An especially memorable trauma sufferer was a boy named Roberto. One morning, he went on a tear of destructive behavior in his second-grade classroom, turning over desks, ripping papers off bulletin boards, swearing at his teacher, and terrifying his classmates. The teacher cleared the classroom by moving students to a neighboring class, then called an emergency code that rang every phone in the office. When I heard all those phones ringing, I knew a crisis was occurring.

In a matter of moments, my day was turned upside down. I made a call over the school's public address system, requesting members of the trauma team to report to the front office. These staff volunteers, who had been trained in crisis prevention, arrived quickly. We devised a plan of response to help Roberto peacefully leave the classroom and get to my office. I emphasized, as I always do in these situations, we only place our hands on a child if he is going to hurt himself or someone else. The moment, and I mean the moment, you place your hands on a child in the midst of traumatic fight, flight, or freeze response, you forever change your relationship with that child and that child's feelings about school.

A Servant Leader Example: "Are You Done?"

When we peeked into the classroom door, it looked as if an earthquake had targeted just one of our twenty-four classrooms. Roberto and his teacher were separated by at least ten feet. I looked in, locked eyes with him, and asked if the two of us could talk. He gave me a calm nod. I gave him a thumbs up, went outside to my team, and dismissed them. I asked if he was ready to make the walk to my office to relax and talk when he was ready. He nodded his consent, so I said, "Let's go."

Although I knew Roberto by name, as I did all 350 students at school, I also knew a bit more. The local office of the state's Division of Families and Children had been in contact with me a few weeks prior to this event. There was a report of suspected abuse, which our school adjustment counselor, Sue Delahunt, and I followed up on. This included interviewing Roberto and his younger kindergartener sister, which went nowhere. It was evident to Sue and me that Roberto and his sister had been told not to share anything with the school.

As Roberto and I walked into the hallway, he immediately sprinted away from me. I sighed to myself, instantly frustrated that I had dismissed my team. I was left to track down Roberto alone. I saw him dart into an enclosed staircase that led to the second floor. I got to the door and yanked it open, already preparing myself to take the stairs two at a time. BOOM! There was Roberto, standing and waiting for me. He had punched me right in the chest as hard as he could. He only weighed about seventy-five pounds, so I wasn't injured but was surely startled.

Both of us were breathing heavily. His fists were clenched. Angry, slow tears slipped out at the corners of his eyes and snot ran from his nose. I was momentarily stunned and upset with myself for thinking I could handle this situation alone. My ego was still in need of being checked.

I had to treat this student the way he needed to be treated. This called for me to be in service to him and address his needs over mine. I could have said any number of things to Roberto, including reprimanding him, blaming him for the disruption he caused, framing the incident from my perspective, or shaming him for the hurt and harm he had caused. I could have said, "Roberto, you cannot tear up your classroom, run from your principal, and then hit him in the chest. You're in big trouble, young man!"

None of those responses would have come from a place of empathy—understanding better through perspective taking or dignity in response. None of them would allow him to maintain his feelings of self-worth. Reacting punitively to a situation such as Roberto's serves only the person in charge, who can self-righteously hide behind rules of school and unnecessarily apply consequences that only do further harm.

Roberto was waiting for my response. I hoped I had found the right words when I calmly asked, "Are you done?" No judgment, no punishment, just a question. It was like taking the air out of a balloon. His fists opened, his heavy breathing slowed, and he wiped his eyes and nose. I extended my hand and he took it. We walked the remaining twenty-five feet to my office, holding hands.

In all cases in which children experience fight, flight, or freeze behaviors, they are communicating need through their actions. By choosing empathy, I had actively recognized a student's distress, which allowed me to separate my ego from the situation in real time. Even being hit wasn't about me; it was about Roberto and how completely out of control he was feeling.

When we made it to my office, I offered Roberto a place to decompress and to talk only when he was ready. He took a seat in one of my kid-sized chairs and started to cry. I waited for him to stop before I asked, "Are you ready to talk?"

Dignity waits; it doesn't demand. So, when he was ready, I asked my student that very important question that my former fifth grader Adam taught me: "Tell me, has something changed at home or at school that you'd like to talk about?" As all educators know, the answer in situations like these is almost always "yes," but the student might not be willing to talk about it right then.

Roberto described the abuse he and his younger sister were receiving from their mother and her boyfriend. They were being locked in a closet at night, so their mother and her boyfriend could use drugs and then cut the rest to sell. He had a lot to say, and I had a lot to comprehend, plan, and now do something about. I listened and stayed composed, although it was difficult to do.

When he was finished with his story, I escorted him to the nurse's office so he could rest, and I could get to work. In service to this one student out of 350, I now was committed to reporting his abuse. I was not treating Roberto like all the other students (equally). I was giving all of my time to just one student that needed me most (equitably). I called the state's Division of Children and Families, setting in motion this chain of events:

- I talked to a case worker to complete a report.
- On the advice of the case worker, I called the student's biological father, whom I had never met and who lived more than thirty miles away.
- I told the children's father that he had to come and get his kids today or DCF would place them in emergency child protection (foster homes).
- When the father was noncommittal, telling me about his new life with his new girlfriend, I had to clearly state if his children went into DCF care they were likely to face further abuse and neglect. I said, "Sir, come get your children."
- With our school adjustment counselor, I met the father at our school, discussed what had happened, and encouraged him to seek full custody of his children.
- I dismissed Roberto and his sister to their dad.

It was only 11 am, but I still had lots of follow-up required for these two students. This was certainly not a typical school day, but situations like these arose everywhere I taught and led, from urban and suburban poverty to middle class to extreme affluence.

If leaders engage in service to their stakeholders, we should be cognizant of how empathy helps us discover and connect and how dignity maintains self-worth with face-saving strategies at the ready. With a service-first mindset, all leaders will be using their power to empower those in need.

A Purpose to Serve

In his book *Aspire: Discovering Your Purpose Through the Power of Words*, Kevin Hall wrote, "Your gifts are not about you. Leadership is not about you. Your purpose is not about you. A life of significance is about serving those who need your gifts, your leadership, your purpose."

Hall's quote encapsulates many of my ideas about servant leadership. Further tapping into the empathy you feel and the dignity you allow supports a leadership of serving. When leaders strive to serve all students, no matter their situation, it helps create more equitable school cultures.

Couple this with a growth mindset that believes everyone can improve their abilities, talents, and intelligence and you have an improved direction for equity. Because there is no way to become fully successful or inclusive as a school or society without focusing on equity, I will present a path forward for schools to make good on our country's promise for life, liberty, and the pursuit of happiness for all through an effective education for all.

There are plenty of hard discussions to hold within school communities on equity, but discussion is not enough. Schools have to dig deep, review the data, and discover a new, more informed way to deliver education so that all students are presented with opportunities to learn, grow, and become valued members of the school community. That's a topic I'll be examining in depth in chapter 6.

Reflections on How Life Should Be

- A head and heart leader must learn to say, "I take responsibility," no matter what's happening.
- An effective leader understands that being right is overrated. Whether the leader is right or not is of little consequence when a teacher is crying, a child has flipped a table, or a board member is demanding a favor for a constituent.

- I have always told my school staff members, "What we do for the least of us, we do for all of us." Everybody watches when we stop, notice, and care for those who have less, socially, cognitively, economically, physically, or emotionally.
- Terry Roller, the chief administrative officer for the Alabama State Department of Education, said, "As a servant leader who acts with humility and empathy, it's always my job to find and provide whatever children and adults need to become successful."
- If we are to tap into servant leadership, we should be cognizant of how empathy helps us discover and connect and how dignity maintains self-worth for our stakeholders.

6

Equity's Promise

Perhaps my most positive experience with a school culture that focused on equity was during my tenure as principal of the Fiske School. In community-wide meetings, individual classrooms, and parent communication, we repeatedly made student inclusion a topic of discussion. Beyond just telling our students inclusion was important, we modeled and celebrated inclusionary practices. We also noticed when students weren't upholding our values (fair, inclusive, safe, kind, and encouraging) by acting in exclusionary ways. We would ask them what happened, what value they broke, what was the result of their actions, and what they needed to change or learn in order to uphold our values.

If you do the head work necessary to build the processes and procedures that lead to an "all means all" school culture, you'll begin to notice heart-focused moments of true inclusion will follow. Positive results aren't always immediately evident, of course, or even measurable. But I can tell you that on those occasions when I observed our students living out our school values for inclusion, it always warmed my head and heart.

One of those positive, equity-building moments occurred on the playground on a sunny spring day. During recess, I noticed three third-grade girls on a climbing structure, smiling and playing with their classmates. There was nothing new there, but for the first time that school year, the girls, two immigrants from Somalia and another from Iraq, were wearing their traditional Muslim headdresses.

I couldn't help but smile, too, as I watched them play with classmates. When I later asked these three how everyone in school had responded to their new choice to wear hijabs at school, they told me they'd received polite and interested questions. It seemed their classmates were interested in understanding the meaning of their hijabs. That memory of inclusivity is one of my prouder leadership moments from Fiske.

Sadly, not all symbols of difference are accepted. In fact, only a year after I left the Fiske School, a parent circulated an anti-Muslim image through email to the school community. Equity is fragile and susceptible to hatred and ignorance. This why true equity requires constant practice and leadership's vigilance to identify signs of exclusion.

Intention and Practice

At the Fiske School, our intentions were clearly defined in all that we did and how we refined and improved practices each year. Our goal was to help each student feel like an integral community member by delivering on our promises. This meant understanding what the larger community required to achieve equity but also coming through for individual students in ways that mattered to them.

Sammy, the student I mentioned in chapter 2, needed more services than our school could provide, but I wanted him to still feel connected to the community that loved him. That's why I made his attendance at our after-school program a priority, and walked him from his van into school each day, when the van driver said he could not. This was a promise I made for equity's sake.

Even before his out-of-district school placement occurred, psychologist Sharon Grossman and I regularly checked in with his second-grade classmates by providing updates when he was absent. With permission of Sammy's mother, Sharon and I shared a little bit about one of his lengthy out-of-school absences for a medical evaluation. This class consistently amazed us with their compassion and empathy. Students often said things like, "He's part of our family, and we miss him." "What can we do to let Sammy know we still love him?" "When will Sammy be back?" One time, under their own direction, the students created and sent cards to Sammy.

Because dignity and empathy are so closely aligned for servitude, compassion must be present if schools are to be truly equitable. Compassion takes us from the emotions of the heart in perspective-taking to the planning of our heads, because leaders act on what's best for an individual to groups of students. Sharon and I didn't meet with every class when students were out for absences beyond a few days, but for Sammy and his class it was important that we did so.

Limitation through Expectations

When I make presentations at schools and conferences across the country, I tell my authentic stories of challenges as well as successes. My willingness to share difficulties often encourages participants to tell their own stories of how equity's promise has failed to include them.

At one presentation, a superintendent in the audience asked to share a story with the group. A highly capable Black woman, currently preparing to defend her doctoral thesis, she recalled a painful story from her undergraduate years. During an English class, the professor had called on her, the only Black student in class, to read a poem written by a Black poet. When she finished, the professor told her, "Not like that. Read it, you know, the other way." He was asking her to read in Black dialect for this class of white students.

That something like this happened just a few years ago reminds us that negative stereotypes don't just exist in our educational system, but that we are often the ones reinforcing them. Consider these sobering statistics:

- Black and Latino student are consistently underrepresented in advanced placement classes.[1]
- Women receive only 21 percent of bachelor's degrees in engineering.[2]
- Students identifying as gay, lesbian, or bisexual attempt suicide up to five times higher than their heterosexual peers.[3]
- Black students' out-of-school suspension rates are more than twice their population whereas white students' rates are underrepresented.[4]
- Black students made up 26 percent of New York City's schools, yet were about 52 percent of all the students suspended in one school year.[5]

The first step we can take to change these telling data points that represent millions of schoolchildren is to raise our own awareness of what's happening in subtle and overt ways. And a good way to do that is to learn about some of the incredible work being done by many forward-thinking social psychologists, including Stanford University social psychologist Dr. Claude Steele.

Expectations Matter

Dr. Steele is the author of *Whistling Vivaldi: How Stereotypes Affect Us and What We Can Do.* He's spent his career studying what he calls the "stereotype threat," the idea that people who are constantly presented with stereotypes about their social group can be more likely to conform to those very stereotypes. Examples include the low percentages of females in advanced math classes; parents who tell their children, "We're not an artistic family"; or Black students who are discouraged from enrolling in AP classes. According to Dr. Steele, when educators have lower expectations of students, students will go along and perform to those low bars. The teachers see the results they expected to see, and the students remain stuck in a stereotype threat that negatively affects their lives.

Such a threat was part of the problem Dr. Adrian Mims, founder of The Calculus Project, realized when he observed such a small percentage of Black students taking AP math courses and then dropping the course the first time they experienced failure, as shared in chapter 2. The threat wasn't stated by any educator, but it was felt in the environment in which Black students weren't expected to take or succeed in AP math courses. If they received a poor grade early in the year, teachers usually didn't offer assistance but instead encouraged the students to drop the classes, saving themselves the hard work of helping a student break through the existing stereotype threat. Students also were willing to protect their grade point averages by earning stronger grades in classes they could easily pass.

In Dr. Steele's original research, he "tested" college students during a round of miniature golf.[6] For a group of white students, researchers told them the game was a measure of their natural athletic abilities. With this information, the group felt the pressure of trying to outperform the stereotype that white kids were not naturally athletic. The result was this experimental group performed three shots worse than the white control group.

In a cohort of Black students, Dr. Steele's researchers told the experimental group that the game was a test of their athletic intelligence. With these students feeling the threat of stereotype that Black kids aren't smart, they performed four shots worse than the Black control group.

Further research found that the threat of stereotypes are so deeply ingrained that even answering a demographic question about ethnicity before taking a standardized test negatively affected test scores.

Today and Tomorrow

Today. Take time to study school-wide practices of inclusion and exclusion. Use data such as suspension rates for different student populations, which students are in remediation versus advanced classes, or heterogenous student groupings that are successful. Take a three-step approach for data study: (1) Make it graphically large, (2) start discussions by accepting only factual responses to the data set, and then (3) encourage curious and concerning questions to drive discussion and allow "why" questions.

Tomorrow. Make equity part of your daily mission in all that happens in your school. Seek out educators who will be early adopters for innovation. Develop plans intently while trying to determine roadblocks that could stop changes in their tracks. Build capacity slowly and accept the new directions these initiatives take you, because tackling what's urgent usually brings up other important factors to study and address.

Educate Students or Discipline Hairstyles?

Students have been disciplined, even barred from high school graduation, for their hats, hoods, piercings, hair color, and clothing choices. When I visited an alternative high school in Sapulpa, Oklahoma, I was standing in the hallway, talking with the principal. A student with bright blue hair walked by. The principal called the student by name, and they both waved and smiled. I asked the principal if he thought students' hair color affected their learning or disrupted the learning environment. "No," he said, scoffing at the notion.

Beyond minor infractions that are easily overblown, when students' opportunities are limited by their religion, race, ethnicity, sexuality, disability, and gender, we are actually limiting our communities and the world's health and well-being. Students who could become productive members of a democratic society by positively participating in civic, economic, and social lives are discounted by the bias districts, schools, and teachers hold against them. Head and heart leaders need to check themselves to see if their jobs have primarily become ones of policing their schools for fashion infractions. Their energy could instead be directed to much more productive purposes.

Check Yourself for Implicit and Explicit Bias

Two kinds of biases—implicit and explicit—place populations seen as "others" at odds with adults who create the unfair rules to keep the social order in place. Biases that are implicit gain widespread acceptance simply because leaders and teachers don't understand how rules, regulations, statistics, or societal norms contribute to subconscious stereotypes about some student populations. This can manifest itself in collective shoulder shrugs when school data teams look at school discipline data that show Black students getting suspended at a rate two times that of other student populations. This can also show itself in teacher course recommendations that leave certain social groups out of college prep classes while overloading the same students in remedial courses.

Biases can range from students being called racial epithets to the creation of policies to keep students out of classes, clubs, sports teams, and school altogether. Some students will actively fight against adult actions by protesting, breaking school norms, or acting in ways seen as disrespectful. Schools respond by punishing the students' action and agency even further.

There are two steps of inequity. First, schools create the unfair conditions that some students will see as an affront that requires a response to maintain self-worth and determination. Then the school penalizes students for fighting back. It's an imbalance of power through bias, both implicit and explicit.

Belief Becomes Reality

Failing to make good on equity's promise means we might lose a scientist who discovers cleaner energy, a chef at a Michelin-rated restaurant, or a plumber who helps get your hot water back. All it can take is that one inspirational teacher, principal, or counselor to invest in a child, the way Coach Richards did for chief administrative officer for the Alabama State Department of Education Terry Roller in chapter 5. If schools turn their backs on equity, students can become hopeless without viable skills and strategies to join the workforce and ultimately become sad, lonely people who lack passion and purpose.

Dr. Mims, a former dean of Brookline High School, drew on his own love of math as a way to empower more Black and Brown students to excel in advanced-level math classes. Mims and his staff members wanted to show their students the possibilities a strong math foundation can provide in whatever they chose to do. The Calculus Project believes in the achievement potential of Brown and Black students, whose families are poor, and who attend chronically underfunded city schools. The belief has become a reality for many.

Many go on to pursue math careers. Quite a few become math teachers. In fact, as part of The Calculus Project Leadership Academy summer program, high school students tutor the younger middle schoolers. Amazingly the program's juniors and seniors not only take the Massachusetts Middle School Math Teacher exam but also they pass this adult teacher test at a rate of 75 percent, better than prospective teachers, who pass at a rate of 65 percent.[7] For Dr. Mims, the point is that he can teach Black and Brown students not only to excel in math and peer tutor younger students but also to do so in a manner that meets and exceeds the standards meant for adult teachers. As a result, several of his first peer tutors have become math teachers.

Mindset Moment

When I taught fifth grade, I wore a special tie on the first day of school with a child's drawing of different professions: artist, chef, police officer, judge, athlete, and dancer. I talked to my students about how I wanted to help them to become whatever they wanted to become. I let them know that with hard work, a fulfilling life was possible.

Twenty years after teaching my first class, I decided to look up my former students, who were now almost thirty years old. In many cases, my belief had been realized. I found a soloist in the Boston Ballet, a mentor helping poor students graduate college, an office manager for a network of dental offices, a lawyer, and a medical student.

This follows the course of an equity-based learning culture, in which Dr. Mims and his team act on the beliefs, mindsets, behaviors, and narratives that feed a culture of growth with a continuation of successes. Dr. Mims and his team model a growth mindset and believe these students can achieve at high levels, regardless of experience, economic standing, or skin color. He also provides support to all stakeholders—students, teachers, families, and the schools.

Head and heart leaders see the opportunities inside challenges and work on ways to reach all students. They do not bemoan matters over which they have no control, such as family incomes, homelessness, second language needs, or how much students read at home. They understand there is a world outside their school doors, and they can only control what happens inside their schools. They use cultures of growth in believing students can achieve then creating the conditions of support for teachers and students to meet those beliefs with tangible and successful results. This mindset ensures a culture based on improvement, no matter how challenging it can be to attain.

The Story of Sunnyside

Sunnyside, Washington, is a three-hour drive east of Seattle, sitting on an elevated desert that Meriwether Lewis and William Clark called their "Eden" on their westward trek from St. Louis to the Pacific Ocean. It's a small agriculture-based community with large percentages of poor, non-native English speakers, many of whom pick fruit in season from the area farms.

In the early 2000s, Sunnyside School District was struggling mightily and so were the district's seven thousand students. High school graduation rates hovered at about 40 percent, unemployment was rising, and gang violence increased. The high school principal attended three student funerals for gang-related deaths in one semester.

School leaders could no longer accept a 60 percent non-graduation rate and neither could the community. Central office staff members and building leaders developed a multifaceted plan to address the crisis. Only one leader was changed during this time, so the people responsible for the dreadful graduation rates would also be the ones in charge of changing course. The team took these actions:

- Partnering with nearby Gonzaga University for support
- Restoring relational trust with all stakeholders
- Rewriting the curriculum for greater interest and engagement
- Adopting a growth mindset approach in teaching, leading, and learning

There were thousands of other steps leadership took on the journey to committing an entire school community to greater achievement and learning. Their goal was simple and challenging—graduate 100 percent of their students. The mission started in pre-K and extended to all eight schools in the district.

When I visited Sunnyside to address all staff members to kick off the school year, it was after the school had devoted a decade of hard work to their goal. (By the way, all staff members meant *all*, including cafeteria, transportation, and maintenance departments in addition to educators.) Graduation rates had risen from that low-water mark of 40 percent to 90 percent. Small and poor Sunnyside was graduating students at the same rate as Bellevue, Washington, schools, home of Microsoft and all the revenue and resources that come along with parents who work there and live in those neighborhoods.

Even after reaching 90 percent, Sunnyside's work continued. When I spoke with school leaders about why they wanted to hear my message on a growth mindset, I was told they weren't done. They were still keeping their eyes on that 100 percent graduation rate prize. Then-superintendent Dr. Richard Cole told me, "We have about thirty-five kids who didn't graduate last year. We know them all by name, and we know what they need. We still haven't given up on them."

Cole readily admitted that it was a long process to get everyone to believe in their students. It took failures to learn from, lots of time for collaboration, and successes to celebrate. It also required putting those beliefs into action, from Cole meeting families in the fields where they were harvesting crops to teachers taking time to know each of their students' needs.

Robert Bowman, a passionate, fast-talking, and affable leader, was the principal of Sunnyside's Harrison Middle School during my initial keynote and subsequent school visits. He used his belief in all students to create intentional, equitable plans that supported growth and learning for students, wherever they happened to land on the academic spectrum. (Bowman is now superintendent in neighboring Naches Valley School District.)

Studying Performance, Reaching All

During Sunnyside's efforts to change, Bowman and his administration team studied student performance for all one thousand sixth through eighth graders, categorizing them into six different areas of support by comparing grades from one quarter to the next. His goal was to find student needs and then provide the means for each student to improve. The student categories were as follows:

- *Critical need*—going down two letter grades or more in two or more classes

- *Need*—students who declined one letter grade in two or more classes
- *Unchanged*—learning at expected rates
- *Improved*—improvement of half a grade or more in two classes
- *Close to 4.0*—GPAs 3.7–3.9
- *4.0*—Straight As

Bowman and his team provided different, equitable levels of support for each student. Students who fell in the "critical need" category were individually seen by Bowman and counselors. They were asked, "We noticed your grades have gone down this past quarter. What's going on?" Bowman said students' answers usually included homelessness, hunger, transience, divorce, abuse, or drug and alcohol use in the home.

The levels of support included connecting students with an in-school mentor, strategically placing them into weekly advisory groups with the most empathetic adults in school, and accessing wraparound health services within the community. Mentors were asked to create relationships with critical-need students whenever they were available, listen to them, and become a point person for academic and emotional support. For students at all levels, the key was listening. Mentors were encouraged to spend the time and have the willingness to listen for understanding without jumping to respond.

Students landing in "need" or "unchanged" categories had academic support systems in place to provide extra help. Harrison staff members met with them individually or in small groups to provide the incentive that happens when a teacher notices and gives advice for improvement.

The two higher academic categories—"close to 4.0" and "4.0" students—were motivated by recognition and validation. Students who improved that half a letter grade, which included moving from a C to C+, also met with teachers at school to discuss their growth, wherever it occurred on the grading scale. Two teachers volunteered for this all-day duty and were provided substitute teachers to do so. Similar to critical need students, teachers took notice of half-grade improvements in two or more classes and asked, "How were you able to improve?"

Bowman says teachers received answers that varied from students changing study habits to not hanging around with students who were not helpful. But the number one answer was that a teacher had taken the time to stop, notice, and provide support during class or on the teacher's own time. Bowman reports kids would say things like, "Mrs. Smith just wouldn't give up on me. She told me to come before school for help if I could."

Student feedback on improvement from individual meetings was also shared at school-wide faculty meetings, so providing extra support became socially normed. Teachers often told Bowman that hearing these stories was the best day of teaching in their careers because all they heard were a constant stream of success stories.

Students close to a 4.0 GPA were asked, "What did you need to get to a 4.0?" Photographs of students with 4.0 grades were posted on school walls. These students and their families were also invited to an evening banquet for their families, when teachers would further praise their students. The 4.0 banquets expanded from one night to four, to accommodate so much improvement.

Changing the System to Help Students Do Better

Most schools can identify students with poor grades and high flyers, but Bowman says it's taking time for students in the middle that's uncommon. "There's nothing in place to honor kids hovering in the middle who just need a little bit of affirmation that they can move from a C to a B." Through this system of equitable support, Bowman's students reached higher levels of achievement, supported by policies, procedures, pedagogy, and decision-making that lead to more opportunity for all, such as shown by these reforms:

- Grading for academic achievement only and removing obstacles such as factoring participation, homework, or behavior into grading
- Replacing F grades with I grades—for insufficient evidence to grade students
- Allowing students with I grades the whole quarter or school year to make up their work for grading
- Providing retakes to improve grades

These changes bucked traditions that had been one hundred years in the making. And none of the changes was made lightly and without disagreement. The pushback from staff members on allowing students extra time and test retakes centered on the timeliness that is required in life for activities such as arriving on time to board a plane or a buying a home.

Some staff members felt they might be letting kids off the hook and encouraging a lack of responsibility by providing extra time.

Timing Matters

Bowman doesn't think he would have been as successful in taking on the challenge of categorizing and supporting a whole school earlier in his career. Back then, he wasn't good at prioritizing, and it was an effort with many competing priorities. Urgent matters always came up, and important ones could slip by because it was possible to put them off. The key, he found, was choosing what was most urgent and creating the systems to support it.

With permission from the superintendent's office, he connected his system of categorization and support to the school mission. He also worked with his administrative team to make sure categorizing his students was even possible. By doing so, he found questions and misconceptions staff members might have about the process, such as what if a student went down two grades in one class, but was unchanged in all other classes? Beyond meeting with students, Bowman also taught an advisory group, as did every adult in school, including office help, teaching assistants, and custodial staff members. Modeling the struggles of teaching an advisory group opened the door for Bowman to ask lots of questions and ask his staff members for help.

The realization that all that work was having a positive effect occurred when Bowman overheard two sixth graders talking about going to after-school tutoring. When one student balked at going, her friend said, "Wait, why wouldn't you want to improve your grade? Come on, it's only twenty minutes, and I'll be there." It was music to Bowman's ears, because middle schoolers are far more affected by their peers than by adults in their lives. When peers began to convince one another to strive and succeed, he knew his plan was making an impact.

Everything that happened at Harrison Middle School was based on research conducted to determine the three factors of a middle school experience that leads to a greater risk for dropping out of high school. This included high absenteeism, a poor behavior grade, and failing either math or reading.[8] Because middle school mattered for eventual high school success, Bowman had the blessing of district leadership to create innovative plans and measures to help all Harrison students.

Active Participation Supports Equity's Promise

For many students, schools are the first place they feel the sting of inequities. Beyond reading, writing, and arithmetic, America's ideals and dichotomies collide in classrooms where students can be counted on or counted out before they turn eighteen years old. Making good on equity's promises in school means doing what is necessary for the individual students and for the collective at school and in society. Inspiring and normalizing the work of equity is the duty of the head and heart leader. Leaders use their head in modeling how to help a student in need or creating improved systems of support through an entire school or district. They use their hearts in understanding that the equity experience at their schools may be far from ideal and then in having the courage to address what's happening and what needs to change.

Elevating equity to a priority comes with complexities in recognizing, addressing, planning, assessing, and adjusting how classrooms function and schools respond to inequities, which can exist in every school. The practicality of delivering on equity and inclusion isn't necessarily the challenge but in how leadership prioritizes and plans for it. There's no way to anticipate all the cultural landmines that will present themselves through changes, but leaders who actively participate in all aspects of the necessary steps along the way put themselves in places of authority by simply being there to gauge how it's going. This requires asking questions such as the following:

- What is best for students?
- What biases—both implicit and explicit—do our class, department, school, or district hold that hurt students' opportunities for a full life?
- Does our equity rhetoric match school actions?
- Are policies, procedures, or pedagogy getting in the way of some students achieving at the very highest levels?
- If we uncover systemic racism, how do we remedy it?
- What is our call to action and our evaluation to create more equitable schools?

If school leadership is unwilling to tackle the hard work of identifying those practices and becoming more equitable, schools will never tap the potential for every child. The work is hard, the challenges many, and true equity calls for intentional planning with plenty of opportunities for growth in children and adults. Staff members, students, and the community will appreciate when everyone feels like a viable member of a community.

An effective head and heart leader helps shape the shared narrative of each class, department, school, or district. In a leader's hands, the headaches and heartaches can be crafted into the narratives of stakeholder growth as stories to be shared over and over again.

In chapter 7, I highlight the integral part that narrative plays in culture curation. Everything a leader does contributes to organizational story making. The good, the bad, and the indifferent stories will precede you in meetings and plans. It matters how leaders present those narratives through the varying ways of communicating them, from walking in the hallways of school to answering questions at school board meetings. In chapter 7, we learn the effects, consistency, and clarity of what leaders say and how they say it.

Reflections on How Life Should Be

- Because dignity and empathy are so closely aligned for servant leadership, compassion must be present if schools are to be truly equitable.
- Dr. Claude Steele, author of *Whistling Vivaldi: How Stereotypes Affect Us and What We Can Do,* studies "stereotype threat," the idea that people who are constantly presented with stereotypes about their social group can be more likely to conform to those very stereotypes.
- The Calculus Project's Dr. Adrian Mims follows the course of an equity-based learning culture, acting on the beliefs, mindsets, behaviors, and narratives that feed a culture of growth with a continuation of successes. Dr. Mims and his team believe their students can achieve at high levels, regardless of experience, economic standing, or skin color, and he enlists parents as allies.
- In Sunnyside, Washington, middle school principal Robert Bowman found ways to provide different, equitable levels of support for each student in the school, which in turned helped the high school raise graduation rates from 40 percent to 90 percent.
- There's no way to anticipate all the cultural landmines that will present themselves through changes, but leaders who actively participate in all aspects of the necessary steps along the way put themselves in places of authority by simply being there to gauge how it's going.

Messages Matter

A favorite author of mine, Joan Didion, writes, "We tell ourselves stories in order to live."[1] Storytelling is as critical as food, water, shelter, and love. I asked you in chapter 3 to describe a teacher or coach who had a significant impact on your life. If I ask you to tell me a story about that person, you'll likely have one. It might be a story about overcoming an embarrassment, learning something challenging, or being validated. If you think beyond school, there are moments big and small that have provided the foundation and backdrop for meaning in your life and stories you can share.

Not everyone is born a gifted storyteller, but you can learn to become one. Whether through speaking or writing, you'll have plenty of chances to improve at school events or through written communications. No matter what, you'll have to write. If you're apprehensive about putting words down, just remember that your writing will improve the more you do it. As bestselling author Stephen King said, "I want to suggest that to write to your best abilities, it behooves you to construct your own toolbox and then build up enough muscle so you can carry it with you. Then, instead of looking at a hard job and getting discouraged, you will perhaps seize the correct tool and get immediately to work."[2]

All you need is a willingness to share and show the value of teaching, learning, and leading. Here are some helpful hints to get you started:

- Look for and honor small, meaningful moments because they can lead to effective stories and they happen every day.
- Make connections to those you serve and relay stories about common interests and experiences.

- Practice writing, speaking, and presenting. There is no substitute for rewriting, taking words out, putting some in, or practicing your remarks aloud before stepping up to a microphone.
- Find your style. Mine includes a love of ellipses, the repetition of key words at least twice when speaking, and the composition of staff email messages and family newsletters.
- Emphasize your mission or values often. There are many opportunities to stay on mission in what you say or write.

The Israeli conductor-turned-consultant Itay Talgam talks about the importance of recognizing multiple contributors in his TED Talk "Lead Like the Great Conductors." He stresses that storytelling includes not just the leader's story but also the stories that are shared with the conductor from the orchestra, audience, instrument makers, concert hall builders, and all the individuals who participated in the concert's creation, as well the audience. During a concert, the conductor has a strong hand in shaping the musical message, but the narratives grow only richer and deeper when all stories are considered.

It's Always a Good Time to Tell a Story

As with culture curation, the leader's job is to gather stories of the students, staff members, and families and share them everywhere they can be told. Stakeholders never will be able to get behind leaders who don't share themselves. For leaders, this means it's better to reveal who you are, including what you honor, what you value, and what encourages you. These stories also live in their followers, so leaders who create narratives and share what's important gather momentum in their stakeholders joining and adding to what eventually becomes a story of the collective "us."

Where to Share

Your readers and listeners aren't expecting a page-turning thriller or beautiful sonnet, but they will expect consistency of message, something that makes them smile, an acknowledgment, a nod to those you serve, plans for the future, a response to a crisis, or the warmth of community that connects all stakeholders in common purpose. Your places for storytelling are only limited by what you want to try. Messages, from bite-sized vignettes to longer compositions or videos, are easy to capture on a phone or tablet. Here are some places to post your stories:

- *Social media*—from photos with brief captions to threads started to engage discussion
- *Email*—an old stalwart for longer messages, links to newsletters, or important news
- *Newsletters*—sent home in backpacks or, better, posted online
- *Automated calls home*—seemed to dissipate with the advent of smartphones, but a voice heard is sometimes better than words read
- *Videos*—from social media to your own online channels; carry greater weight with students and families in a form that can be easily digested and go viral
- *Text messaging*—quick notes, usually reserved for only the most important communication and not the proper medium for storytelling
- *Community meetings and assemblies*—whether with just students and staff members or including families, offer opportunities to share values on a wider scale
- *Staff meetings*—used as a way to make space for everyone's storytelling, not share information that could be sent by email
- *In the hallways, classrooms, and conference rooms*—leaders seeing, talking, messaging, or meeting with staff members presents an opportunity to communicate mission, values, or vison; using each and every one of these chance or planned exchanges can infuse the collective narrative of "us"

It will be interesting to experience how these methods may continue to evolve over time, but we can agree that communicating—at least sending out a message—has never been easier. Of course, communication takes a sender and receiver ready to read, listen, or see the message. Leaders have to use methodologies to create excitement and anticipation for receiving messages. In this chapter we will examine two different leadership styles separated by thousands of miles and two entirely different communities. But these two leaders' effectiveness is tied to a commitment to define and share what it means to be part of a specific community.

Meet Dr. Hickey

My son is a student at Austin Preparatory School in Reading, Massachusetts. I've heard the school's headmaster, Dr. James Hickey, speak many times. I also read the messages he emails to families. Whether it's a parent meeting, a fundraiser for a new sports fields, or an update on the coronavirus, Dr. Hickey is masterful in connecting his words to the school's Augustinian mission of *veritas, unitas,* and *caritas*—truth, unity, and love.

As the leader of a small, independent Catholic middle school and high school of about 750 students, Dr. Hickey bestows an air of confidence and authority at a lectern or through email. His words are carefully chosen, and they also are heartfelt in communicating with clarity the mission and values of Austin Prep. He holds his audiences' attention, not by entertaining them but by staying on message every time.

The first time I heard Dr. Hickey speak was when he was explaining the new dining hall layout and lunch payment policy. He used the occasion to take what might have been a dry topic and make connections to the school's mission by describing how students would now sit in circular tables with limited seating, making it easier to form stronger relationships at lunch; how the dining hall could host school events; and how incorporating lunch fees into tuition costs could save time for everyone. The new dining hall, he explained, was an extension of *veritas, unitas,* and *caritas,* and it would be a place the school community could grow more effectively and with a great deal of pride.

Dr. Hickey's determination to reinforce values may appear to be effortless, but it's hard work. He told me that he often begins preparing for major addresses many days in advance. Writing, rewriting, and editing are always part of the process.

A political science major in college, he understands that when politicians get tired or bored with repeating their message, that's usually the time it's taking hold and finally being understood. Dr. Hickey knows Austin Prep families are busy and that he doesn't always have a captive audience, so he strategically relies on repetition. This helps set norms for new parents and caregivers entering the community, while reminding everyone else of what matters most at the school. Here's an excerpt from a newsletter when my son first started at Austin:

A few weeks ago, Austin Prep hosted a reception for prospective families prior to a Saturday night performance of the *The Nutcracker* here on campus. At the reception, a parent of an eighth-grade student at another school recounted what her son had said to her after he spent a day with us "shadowing" a ninth grader. Her son came home from Austin Prep that afternoon and said, "There's community there." To me and the Director of Admissions, the parent then asked rhetorically, "What 13-year-old kid would say that, let alone be aware of what community is?" As I engaged in conversation with the parents and the young man, who was blushing a bit as a result of his mom's storytelling, I couldn't help but think that *unitas,* one of our core values at Austin Prep, is apparent even to students in middle school. That eighth grader made his observation because Austin Prep's spirit of community is palpable.

Dr. Hickey stresses leaders have not only a responsibility to communicate but also a platform for it. "In some ways it's like a bully pulpit that Teddy Roosevelt often spoke about. You have the high ground—a box to stand on that no one else has. You can use it to communicate expectations, because your message eclipses everyone else's. This power can promote school culture and values, as well as squash rumors in their place."

Options Are Limitless

It's important to consider what narratives you want to offer and the best places to communicate them. Graphics and pictures consistently grab more attention than just words on social media to communicate or emphasize ideas easily. Even though email rose to popularity with baby boomers and Generation X, it still can be used effectively for more comprehensive messages of greater length. How creative and innovative you become is really up to you. A high school principal you will meet in the last chapter in this book brought in a DJ for the first day of school and had students dance into school in a line with teachers on either side, just like on the music and dance show "Soul Train." She quickly recorded a thirty-second video and posted it on social media only moments after the dance line ended.

Before I was an educator, I was a writer. I love writing because it gives me the opportunity to tell my story with depth and color. Writing is an obvious way most leaders tell stories in all their varied forms. Writing is more personal than speaking because there is something more permanent to words on paper or a screen. Writing takes intention and time to transcribe what's in your head and your heart out to the world, and it can be scary, at first. I always told my fifth graders, "Writing is easy; just lean over the page and bleed." What you're willing to share with your stakeholders is in direct relation to what they'll share back with you.

During my educational career, I was able to combine my passions for education and writing in several ways. My most impactful communication was through emails with my staff members. I emailed them every day. Most of these communications were about where I might be during the day, when I'd be out of the office, a reminder of the day's events, or some general news. On Fridays I sent out my TGIF messages. These were longer, thoughtful missives with stories of what I had seen or felt during the week, something inspirational, meaningful, or just what was top-of-mind for me. These TGIF messages were about five hundred to one thousand words in length, and I did my darndest to hit that send button before the school day started each Friday.

Mindset Moment

Some of my most heartfelt TGIF messages had nothing to do with school. I wrote about my grandmother's sense of humor, my passion for all kinds of music, gardening, my father's death, and the Kentucky Derby. I wrote about how a teacher combed lice from her first grader's hair during recess because family members couldn't or wouldn't, the significance of picture day, and the first record I bought as a kid. Staff members responded to these messages by emailing me back or coming to see me to share stories that connected us. I learned so much about them because I was not afraid to share my whole self.

When I was able to make the time, I wrote the night before Friday for clarity and proofreading. When it came down to the wire, I would be writing as the clock clicked down to Friday's morning bell. I have staff members from every school I led who let me know, "I've kept that TGIF message you wrote about . . . ." See Figure 7.1 for an example of a TGIF message I sent out.

From: Anthony Colannino
Date: Fri, Nov 7 at 8:18 AM
Subject: TGIF
To: WPS-Fiske-Staff

Good morning ...
assemblies today ....
8:45–9:45 all of K and 2M
9:45–10:45 all of grade 1 and 2SV, 2K/M
I have a principal coffee 8:30-9:30.
Here is a rare sighting, a TGIF message:

A few years back there was this great show on PBS—The Dessert Circus—in which a French chef taught you how to make wild stuff like Banana Moon Cakes, Crystal Lollipops, and Chocolate Corn Flakes. There was, of course, circus music and graphics to go along with the show's upbeat theme. It was fun stuff to watch and just dream about making, even if you were just planning to laze around on the couch all day. Ahh, the days before house, children, and dog and going hither and yon, but I digress.

One thing I remember from the show was the chef saying he didn't know why Americans would even think about making brownies from scratch since there were so many box varieties that tasted as good or even better than scratch recipes. And this from a French pastry chef!

Here's the thing about boxed brownies, which I love—my wife makes them better than me. How could this be? I mean, you have the mix, some eggs, oil, and a greased pan. The only thing needed is to mix it all together and bake for the allotted time at the recommended temperature. Just so you know, I do most of the cooking at home, so I wonder where I go wrong or better yet where my wife, Kara, goes right.

I was reminded of this last week when I decided to whip up some brownies while Kara was out at a PTO event at our children's school. I did as I always do, made sure I had the necessary ingredients, preheated the oven, greased the pan, and mixed everything up. The result was OK, but not great, brownies.

Believe it or not, this got me thinking about teaching. With the national push for changes in teacher observation and evaluation (for which we are now catching up) it feels a bit like the brownie mix. The standards are all the mix from which you must choose or are choosing without even realizing it while you teach, the conditions are your classroom, not a preheated oven, and the mixing is what you get when lessons meet your students and they meet you.

The brownies are standardized and the directions, except if you live in high altitude, are standardized as well. Teaching for as much as we want to "standardize" it will never be so, and this is good. The challenge is how to keep the art, yes the art, of teaching healthy and autonomous enough for your and your students' enjoyment and learning while providing a forum of growth for you, us, the students.

I hope you know one of the aspects of the teacher evaluation system I enjoy being part of is the "mix." This is the talking about what you are doing, how you are doing it, and how I can help. Last year in one of my meetings with John D'Auria, he said something so obvious, but something I had not been able to articulate in my ten-plus years of principaling.

He said, "You know Anthony, you're not going to have student growth without adult growth." It was one of these "lightbulb clicking on" kind of moments because it's so true.

I know what good teaching looks like; now I am ever so more committed to improving it along with you. Your teaching, unlike the brownie box, involves something very important that no rubric will ever be able to measure —you. It truly is my joy to help you figure things out, get better, struggle along with you at times because, as we have learned, "failure is just another way of learning."

Thankfully, you all also have that something else that I cannot capture in mixing brownies—your style, verve, and know-how. Some of it you can tell me, other "stuff" can only be witnessed, and some is just your magic with your students.

I know my wife can't tell me how her brownies are better than mine. She can't even show me, but I can taste the difference. For teaching purposes I get to see it and tell you what I see and our conversation ensues. I look forward to it. Maybe I'll bring some brownies.

Have a great weekend,

Anthony

FIGURE 7.1 A TGIF Example

How you communicate is entirely up to you. You can create brief videos on the excitement of learning, pictures with students "getting caught" doing good things, or Facebook posts that highlight a teacher of the week. When you're telling the story of staff members, students, families, and community, you're opening infinite possibilities of hope and growth by not only portraying life in your domain but also showing the incredible value your department, school, or district holds individually and collectively.

Storytelling for Head and Heart

Humans are meaning-makers. It's the reason you bury yourself in a good book, grab the popcorn and watch a movie, or tell a ghost story around a campfire.

Consider our early ancestors of more than forty thousand years ago, who decided to create paint and relate their experience of a hunt on cave walls. These nomads stopped their lives of survival to portray their lives on their available medium: a rock wall. Even though they must have had enough on their minds, such as the constant search for water, shelter, food, and safety, something stirred their imagination to share their stories with their families or those who may happen on their work.

Whether I was speaking in front of my staff members or students, sending out a newsletter, or emailing a response to a crisis, I was letting everyone know what was important or needed to be shared. In this sense, the messaging wasn't about me, it was about what I felt needed to be communicated. As Dr. Hickey demonstrates, any message provides an opportunity to return to a school's mission or values.

The Consistent Leader

The principal of El Paso's Del Valle High School, Antonio Acuña, constantly communicates to make sure everyone understands not only what's going on in school but also why it's important. Del Valle is 99 percent Latinx, with 80 percent of students receiving free or reduced lunch. About two-thirds of his students are categorized as at-risk due to poverty and English language need. Despite this, Del Valle regularly graduates about 95 percent of its seniors. And Acuña knows the first name of every one of the school's 2,100 students.

Acuña doesn't talk about grandiose ideas or lofty plans. Instead, he quietly and efficiently communicates in the hallways, grounds, and through a weekly staff newsletter that's sent at 4 pm every Sunday. How much do staff members look forward to reading Acuña's weekly updates? Recently a teacher called him at 4:05 pm and asked where the newsletter was. Acuña told him to refresh his email. He had sent it at 4:01 pm.

The newsletter's masthead is "Things are impossible until they are not." Dates, announcements, congratulations, and important updates come from high school department heads, school leaders, and administrative assistants. There are no fancy colors or attention-getting headlines. There is only a light nod to graphic design with some clip art and colored boxes. It's a Sunday ritual that helps all prepare for the week ahead.

Don't Promise If You Can't Follow Through

Acuña is consistent in all that he does, whether it's sending a signed card for every student birthday, collecting lesson plans Mondays at 6 pm, or sticking with the same newsletter release time. He doesn't just create expectations—he follows through on them. There are no hidden agendas with Acuña, because all information is out in the open. And most of that information can be gathered by reading his Sunday emails. See Figure 7.2 for an example.

"You have to be consistent," he says, "because if you're not, students and staff members will lose faith in you. They're looking to you and you need to set patterns, protocols, and procedures. If you say you're going to give every student a birthday card on his or her birthday, you have to do it for every single child. You can't miss."

The newsletter always begins with a highlight of someone or a department that has gone above and beyond to meet the needs of the students. By recognizing members of the school, Acuña is curating culture by sharing the limelight, showing love and appreciation, and validating those who serve quietly behind the scenes.

Good Food, Clean Grounds

To gather greater input from his parent community, Acuña started monthly principal coffees. At first attendance was low. Then Acuña asked cafeteria

Things are impossible until they are not

From the Desk of Antonio Acuña
Reset. Reimagine. Respond.

Highlights – This week I would like to highlight our librarian and librarian aides. They played a key role in the distribution of more than 1,000 Chromebooks. We are constantly calling parents to ask for information like parent survey and lunch application. Thank you Mrs. Ortega, Mrs. Nava, and Mrs. Collazo for your flexibility and your positive attitude.

I.   Nov. 2 - Breakfast/Lunch Curbside from 7:00 a.m. to 11:30 a.m. (Open to any students between the ages of 1 and 18)

II.   Nov. 2 - Office hours Monday – Friday 8 a.m. to 4:30 p.m.

III. Nov. 3 - Volleyball - Del Valle vs. Ysleta HS (Home)

IV.   Nov. 3 - Department Head meeting @ 4:15 p.m.

V.   Nov. 4 - Failure report due (Upload)

VI.   Nov. 4 - College Shirt – Please take picture and send it to Mr. Lopez

VII. Nov. 5 - Professional Development – Mr. Medina will send email with details

VIII. Nov. 5 - Counselors meeting at 9 a.m.

IX.   Nov. 5 - Dual Credit meeting

X.   Nov. 5 - Technology Support by appointment only

XI.   Nov. 6 - Friday Schedule – Follow Schedule B today – Snap will be 8th period

XII. Nov. 6 - Volleyball vs. Bel Air HS (Away)

XIII. Nov. 6 - Progress report grades due by 4 p.m.

XIV. Nov. 6 - Football Del Valle Bye Week

FIGURE 7.2   From the Desk of Antonio Acuña

staff members to bake some of their beloved scones for the events, and they delivered with tasty pineapple and pumpkin creations. Sure enough, word got out and attendance increased. When some parents didn't want to voice their concerns publicly, he provided QR codes for family members to share questions privately. The suggestions poured in, and Acuña protected the dignity of family members who weren't comfortable voicing complaints in front of others.

Today and Tomorrow

Today. Find your style, a method, voice, and tone that shows stakeholders who you are and practice writing, speaking, and posting messages for consistency. Walk through your department, school, or district collecting stories you notice and share those anecdotes in however you are communicating. Connect those stories back to mission, vision, or values.

Tomorrow. Create opportunities for all stakeholders to share in storytelling. You can make sure you have places to post stories on bulletin boards in high traffic areas of the school or office space or virtually on school web pages. Give stakeholders the freedom to share their stories directly by creating and posting as part of special weekly or monthly communications. Leaders could also interview stakeholders to gather important information, personally and professionally, that infuses the collective stories of schools.

Even the cleanliness of the high school is a form of communication. Emulating Disney theme parks, Acuña stresses a level of cleanliness that's a point of pride for him, the custodial staff, and ultimately the whole school community. "The majority of our parents will never set foot in our school, but they can see how much we care for it by how clean we keep it from the outside because it's tended to everyday starting at 6 am. It's an older building, but it's always clean and tidy inside and out. In this way, we're showing and telling families we care about their kids."

Acuña and Dr. Hickey create and deliver on ways to communicate with their communities to instill pride, set and follow values, and engage in a dialogue that becomes cyclical in nature. For Acuña, information is taken and used from his weekly newsletter, including staff members congratulating students for winning a game, wishing someone a happy birthday, or providing a reminder of what's coming up. Dr. Hickey knows his messages have resonated when parents cut and paste portions of his messages in emails back to him, reinforcing or supporting what he's shared. These men have two different messaging styles, but both use their heads and hearts to reinforce what it means to be members of their school communities. How you create and execute on messaging is entirely up to you. As long as you build consistency in the execution, you are likely to create followers waiting on your every word.

Banging the Gong: How to Command and Keep Attention

As I highlighted at the beginning of the chapter, there are scores of ways to communicate messages that matter. Whatever forms you use, there are plenty of advantages to consistently sharing messages across platforms. Each medium requires some level of intentionality and practice before becoming comfortable and effective. A few years ago, when automated voice calls became popular where I led, I had to work at speaking slowly and enunciating clearly. When I first started using this tool, I had to record and rerecord messages many times over before getting them right. Eventually I was creating recorded messages so effective that parents told me they'd sometimes hold conversations with my recorded messages, thinking it was actually me.

Find Your Style

How you communicate is an extension of who you are. Unless I was responding to a crisis, I kept most of my messages conversational, with dashes of humor. I could also be considered a bit over-the-top in my exuberance. At community-wide meetings, I juggled anything my students wanted me to, from pumpkins to raw eggs. I wrote and recited an ode to a pig before I kissed her, and once I allowed my students to turn me into a human chocolate sundae. (Those last two forms of communication were rewards for meeting school-wide readathon goals.)

You certainly don't need to use a conversational tone, humor, or exuberance, but you have to find a voice that is yours in every message you share and how you share it. Communicating with formality, authority, dignity, or whatever style becomes most authentic is important, because it will provide your audiences with predictability so they can better understand your message. If you waver or are inconsistent in how you deliver your messages, you'll leave it up to followers to decipher intent while trying to figure out what you're trying to convey.

During my eleven years of school leadership, one of my consistent communications was a weekly newsletter to families. It was straightforward, filled with events, important dates, and possibly a briefer window into the school than my staff TGIF messages. Parents and caregivers would comment that they enjoyed the conversational, welcoming tone and the fun sidenotes. They also appreciated the consistency of receiving something from their children's principal each week. As technology improved, the newsletter moved to online-only delivery. And as redundant as it seems, after posting my online newsletter on our school website, I learned to email families with a link to our website. It was a simple extra step that only cost me a few minutes but increased readership considerably.

Beyond written messages, community-wide meetings were a venue for shared stories for all students to engage in simultaneously, creating and restating our culture. At the first school where I led, community meetings were special occasions, such as the time I allowed the whole school to watch the Red Sox opening day after students met a reading goal. In the second school, these meetings were tied to monthly character traits we focused on, celebrating students and classes that had displayed those traits.

Your Signature Attention-Getting Ritual

When students and teachers began leading community-wide meetings at the MacArthur School, there were only a few elements I controlled, including the attention-getting signal of a simple clap cadence that I started and students repeated. For meeting in such large groups, an attention-getting signal is an important element, not only to start the meeting but also to set the tone. This signal was introduced and practiced when we started these meetings and then reintroduced each year. On those rare occasions when all 350 students didn't pay attention immediately, I waited for quiet before beginning.

Head and heart leaders will understand the value in using a signal to start meetings and use it when they start every meeting on time. Doing this follows Acuña's protocols for communicating by creating predictable and safe patterns for stakeholders to follow.

Your signal can be whatever works for you. Many leaders simply use a raised hand, waiting for audience members to quiet down and raise their hands. Some use a handclap signal or a call-and-repeat saying. For administrative meetings, you can simply call out a two- and a one-minute warning and begin right on time with some general announcements that allow your crowd to quiet down and listen.

Quiet Descends on Dribblers

Can such a simple technique work? Absolutely. If you recall from chapter 2, I wrote about the basketball camp, Shoot Straight, that my father, Joe, started with his friend Mike Jarvis, who had coached NCAA champion and NBA Hall of Famer Patrick Ewing in high school and then went onto to coach at several Division I colleges. I've always remembered how he got a gym full of basketball-shooting kids to listen to him immediately.

On the first day of camp, as hundreds of campers were playing across several gyms, Jarvis would stand at center court in the center gym, blow his whistle with a few, short bursts, and then wait for kids to stop playing and come to center court and surround him. On his first attempt, it would take a few minutes for everyone to stop playing and finally make their way over. He would wait for all the campers to be quiet and then let everyone know for the rest of the camp the moment he blew his whistle, everyone was to stop playing, anyone who had a basketball was to put it in one of two bins on either side of the court, and everyone was expected to run to center court and sit awaiting instructions.

After Jarvis explained this, he told campers that they were going to practice responding to his whistle. He'd send everyone back to shoot around. A minute later, he would blow on that whistle. What had taken several minutes now took about fifteen seconds, as a couple hundred campers responded immediately.

Practice Makes Better

I've used similar techniques for attention-getting wherever I taught and led, and I always started by practicing. This was a matter of respect and validation for all. The message was that our time together was important, that we would use our time wisely, and there was a simple signal to follow. For staff meetings, I used a small gong my mother had purchased at a thrift store. I would provide two- and one-minute warnings before we were to begin, then I would hit the gong three times. By the last gong strike, I expected all staff members to be quiet, facing forward, ready to listen to what I had to say

Just like Jarvis, at our initial meeting, I would let my staff members practice talking and then getting quiet when they heard the gong. From then on, I would use the gong to begin meetings and bring teachers back from activities or opportunities to share. It's important to allow people to interact during meetings, because they are simply too busy during their school days to do so. But without my gong signal to bring them back from their excitement over time spent together, we would have never gotten back on track.

Rinse and Repeat

To lead with head and heart, you must be ready to signal to stakeholders when to speak, when to listen, and how to participate. These consistent, predictable moves are part of what makes messaging matter.

Simple repetitive gestures, mottos, values, or missions that can be repeated clearly and often will provide a clear path for stakeholders to follow. For Dr. Hickey, it's *veritas, caritas, and unitas.* At Del Valle, it's OFOD, which means, One Family, One Destiny. Those messages are repeated on everything from leaders' email signatures to stories delivered at school-wide meetings.

Communicating with Courage

Like it or not, leaders are the faces of their organizations. The story of your leadership is yours to create and share with stakeholders, but it's also the story you first start by telling yourself. Consider how you are creating the conditions for stories to be told and shared. Leaders need to ensure that they are clearly communicating, in good times and in bad. Responses require returning to or exemplifying values, which means more than just messaging but also acting on what's most important to your department, school, or district. When leaders hold stakeholders and themselves accountable is where messaging meets action. Dr. Hickey describes this as "the difficult moments when leaders are the final judges in deciding what it means to live out a mission."

Leaders who message through multiple forms of narrative state and restate their organization's values. Similar to Dr. Hickey, they seize on every opportunity to explain or expand on what makes a department, school, or district special. The message, no doubt, derives from the leader's head and heart in determining what is important or necessary to share, but meaningful messages don't have to always originate from leadership. If leaders are willing only to notice their worlds and then share an anecdote on what was seen, felt, or heard, it carries as much, if not more, weight as whatever comes from a leader's head. In this way, leaders simply become conduits of what is happening all around them.

Said another way, this is where the buck stops and leaders lead. It's also where we will go next in our chapter 8, which is dedicated to courage.

Reflections on How Life Should Be

- In Itay Talgam's TED Talk, "Lead Like the Great Conductors," he says that the narratives grow only richer and deeper when all stories are considered.
- Austin Prep's Dr. James Hickey links all communication back to the school's Augustinian mission of *veritas, unitas,* and *caritas*—truth, unity, and love. He stresses the importance of repetition. A political science major in college, he understands that when politicians get tired or bored with repeating their message, that's usually the time it's taking hold and finally being understood.
- Antonio Acuña, principal of Del Valle High School, sets a standard and follows through on every form of school communication—from a signed birthday card for each student to a weekly newsletter that's delivered promptly at 4 pm each Sunday. "You have to be consistent," he says, "because if you're not, students and staff members will lose faith in you. They're looking to you and you need to set patterns, protocols, and procedures. If you say you're going to give every student a birthday card on his or her birthday, you have to do it for every single child. You can't miss."
- Head and heart leaders understand the value in using a signal to start meetings and use it when they start every meeting on time. Doing this follows Acuña's protocols for communicating by creating predictable and safe patterns for stakeholders to follow.
- Find a voice that is yours in every message you share and how you share it. The story of your leadership is yours to create and share with stakeholders, but it's also the story you first start by telling yourself.

8

Courageous Leadership

'll never forget the moment I realized I was really a homeowner. Just a few weeks after closing on our first house, I was turning on an outside faucet to water the lawn when the knob broke off in my hand. Water spurted everywhere (except on the grass, of course!). And I thought to myself, "I've got to figure out how to fix this." It was a moment when I realized all the responsibility was mine.

When you're in a similar "you and you alone" situation in school, you can sometimes call in an expert, the way I called in a plumber that day. But, just like I felt standing there on my lawn with a faucet knob in my hand, you'll know that, in the end, you're the one who has to summon up the courage to do what's right for your school.

For my first principal gig, I had been hired late in the season and started early August just a few weeks before the start of school. I hustled to make sure the building was shipshape, supplies were delivered, and all students were placed. Following the whirlwind of greeting students and helping dry a few eyes for children and parents on the first day of school, I walked back to my office, asking the school secretary, Debi Tierno, "Now what?"

There was a lot of naiveté and inexperience in my question. And I didn't have to wait long for my first answer in the form a kindergartener sitting outside my office. He was adorable, with his feet dangling from an oversized bench and his chin resting in the palms of his hands. He looked dejected, and it was only a few hours into the school year.

There is no "Students Sitting on the Office Bench" course in the education leadership program I attended. Similar to the broken knob in my hand that belonged on the spigot, I took a few moments to consider my options to figure out how I would return a student back to his class.

I approached cautiously, taking a seat at the other end of the eight-foot-long bench. Instead of questioning him, I decided on a different tactic. I just sat for a few minutes waiting on my first visitor. When he didn't say anything, I asked his name. "Kevin," was the answer. I slid down a little closer. I said, "Kevin, so what's going on?" He offered me a deeply earnest look as he turned his gaze to meet mine, then he replied, "Rules! Rules! Rules!" slapping the back of one hand into the other to emphasize.

It was early in our relationship, but I knew we were likely to spend a lot of time together in the coming days, weeks, and months. This first interaction would help determine our relationship, one that would inform Kevin's kindergarten experience and my leadership style. Following up my initial question and Kevin's response, I asked him to join me in my office for a chat so I could help him figure out what may have gone wrong and how we could fix it.

Courage isn't always undertaken during highly visible moral stands—which hardly occur in schools—but more in the mundane, daily dealings leaders have with colleagues, direct reports, staff members, students, and families. Similar to a muscle, courage needs to be exercised. Ignoring a tug at your head and heart, a feeling, or intuition that demands a courageous response creates uncertainty at best, resentment at worst in your followers.

Wherever you currently lead or eventually want to lead, you'll be presented with conflict and often resolution requires courage. Sidestepping something that requires courage undermines any positive climate, culture, or conditions of learning.

When Doing What's Right Is Also What's Scary

Compounding this challenge is that many of your responses will be clouded with gray areas—interpreting policies and procedures and applying emotions and experiences that may lie outside the lines of standard responses. Leadership decision-making usually isn't contained in lines of section 23, paragraph (a). Agreed-on rules simply can't be applied to every human interaction. Relying solely on rules from a book can be an act of cowardice, because leaders can easily hide behind a policy book instead of using their wisdom to determine what's best given a unique set of circumstances.

Just like a stone creates expanding ripples in water, leaders' decisions will reverberate throughout their culture. The expansion of those decisions will have consequences seen and unseen as well as intended and unintended. How decisions are made and communicated offers all leaders opportunities for curating culture that can expand, because it multiplies in support of growth, or creating unnecessary barriers for betterment. No wonder leaders struggle with choosing what's best or right in decisions big and small.

In chapter 4, I talked about my "free book" plan that unexpectedly blew up in my face when two teachers argued about who should teach *Trumpet of the Swans*. I hadn't yet built up my skills to act with courage, so back then I simply tabled the disagreement for another time, instead of dealing with it effectively in the moment. My unease in remedying that situation in the moment has stayed with me. I learned to be more courageous in instances that required action:

- Upholding values
- Innovating for improvement
- Not taking "no" for an answer
- Apologizing
- Protecting staff members and students
- Consciously rejecting what will hurt staff members, students, and schools
- Maintaining the dignity of all
- Having fun

Any of these circumstances can incite fear or anxiety, even in most experienced leaders. Considering fun, it's necessary for leaders to step out of their comfort zones and summon some sort of courage to crack a smile and plan for their stakeholders to share in one as well. Humor was my shield and my sanity when faced with challenges. A school adjustment counselor, Sue Delahunt, who became a mentor, friend, and confidant used to say, "Colannino, how do you keep smiling and having fun?" The answer is fun was part of who I was and needed to be. It also provided me with opportunities to refocus my energies and enthusiasm for what mattered most.

Love, Joy, and Courage

Kathy Baumgardner, principal of Asbury Park High School in New Jersey, is like a drop of sunshine. She has a bright smile, upbeat personality, and a joy in her voice that's impossible to ignore. No wonder sunshine is part of her Twitter handle. During spring 2015, however, her smile was wiped from her face when her superintendent "voluntold" her to take over the district's struggling high school.

Baumgardner was happy in her current placement as an elementary school principal in the district. Throughout his first two years, the superintendent came back to Baumgardner again and again complimenting her success at the elementary level and remarking that her school was the "flagship" of the district. He noted it as a place where innovation occurred, staff members worked hard, and students enjoyed coming to school. After saying "no" to several different requests, Baumgardner was simply moved to the high school.

At the time, Asbury Park High School was a scary place where food fights, physical altercations, and weapons brought to school were commonplace. Visiting the high school in the spring before she was to take over in the 2016–2017 school year, Baumgardner was astounded to hear a class bell ring and see students remain in the hallway talking, as if they had no classes to attend. She walked back into the office and asked the secretary if a lack of movement to class was typical. "Yes," was the reply and Baumgardner thought to herself, "Why did I agree to do this?"

The virtue of courage and the desire to be courageous is less about bravado, beating of one's chest in the face of fear, and more about how leaders derive and deliver on what's right, especially when it feels scary. Courage is how we face our worries, concerns, and misgivings. Leadership forces you to confront these feelings, because conflict is an incredibly large part of your daily existence in which you'll have to try to land on what's right.

No Bravado Necessary

I have shared stories throughout *Leading with Head and Heart* that required courage: Annette Addair from chapter 4 sharing the vulnerable side of herself with staff members, Robert Bowman from chapter 6 having the audacity to not only remove F grades but also to give students all term or all year to make up work, Kent Bower from chapter 3 using love in words and actions, and Dr. Mims from chapter 2 in his determination to ensure Black and Brown students were given the opportunity to excel in advanced math courses. Along the way, each of these leaders faced self-doubt or obstacles that required a courageous response.

Making it doubly difficult is the fact that what's right or even best doesn't come with a sound effect indicating if you've hit or missed the mark. However, there will be an internal and external barometer of your decisions that will give you an idea of how you did. In the minutes, hours, or days that follow, you will have a feel for what's occurred, and stakeholders involved will react in ways ranging from avoidance all the way through confrontation.

When Baumgardner brought up the idea of starting high school just like she did at the Obama Elementary School, her staff members were resistant. "These aren't elementary school kids," they told her. She persevered and brought a DJ in anyway. Baumgardner knew she had to change the culture of Asbury Park High School, and the best way to start was by curating a new, welcoming culture for students and staff members on the first day of class.

Re-creating the "Soul Train" dance line into school didn't single-handedly reincarnate Asbury Park High into a successful place, but it was a start. It was also a beginning that Baumgardner fretted over, wondering if moving to the high school would be a career killer. Working through self-doubt with a laundry list of school problems, Baumgardner knew she had an opportunity to capture the heads and hearts of her stakeholders if she maintained a high level of joy. This would inform her approach from school discipline to improving course offerings. In all that she did, Baumgardner wanted to make sure she and her staff members made the high school a place students actually wanted to attend.

Mindset Moment

A need for courage will surface wherever you lead. Sometimes what rises up is the need for immediate response with a gravitas necessary to address an issue and then move on.

When I first started as principal at MacArthur Elementary School, staff members often referred to our special education and multilingual learners as "not MacArthur students," because they were drawn from outside our geographic district. With a heart and head for inclusion, I knew that I must address any words or actions that promoted or could lead to exclusionary practices.

During one of my first staff meetings, I asked our cafeteria staff members if I could borrow a milk crate for my staff meeting. Minutes later I told the staff members I had a soapbox I was going to stand on with a one-time announcement they needed to hear. I said, "Any student who walks through our doors is a MacArthur student, and we have the duty and honor to teach that student as long as he or she is our student."

Courage begins by backing your beliefs and your values and then behaving in ways to ensure those beliefs and values are lived and upheld. There are educators and leaders who work in schools where resilience in teaching and learning among extremely difficult circumstances require daily calls for courage. From the ravages of poverty to the ripple effects of trauma to unrelenting demands of parents, educators are constantly called on to behave courageously to ensure an effective education for all their students. Taking it a step further, simply deciding to teach or lead can be taken as acts of courage.

The Talent Show Kerfuffle

Calls for courage can surface in special education team meetings where determining what is right for a student depends on your perspective— parent, teacher, or administrator. It can also arise in how schools remedy societal inequities that seep into and stem from schools' treatment of social groups based on race, religion, ethnicity, or economics. And, yes, courage comes in the little things such as song lyrics for a talent show.

In my first year at Fiske School, I was notified that staff members ran a talent show for grades three through five. A group of teachers volunteered to run the show each year, holding auditions and choosing acts to perform in a school-wide community meeting and an evening show for parents. The first concern I shared with teachers was for them to thoroughly vet songs, not only for inappropriate lyrics but also for song intent. I was reassured that song choice was the chief reason the staff members took over the talent show from parents, who had previously run the show.

Unfortunately, after a few weeks of auditions, and with the chosen acts honing their routines for the show, a fourth-grade teacher came to me with a concern about her discovery of lyrics that might be questionable. She knew, as I did, that if those lyrics were not a fit, multiple parents would need to be told that their children's act would need to be changed if they wanted to continue to participate in the talent show.

In a district of affluence, telling parents "no" is loaded with difficulties. They are often not used to hearing "no" at all. I knew I'd have to make a stand that could potentially land me in the superintendent's office and jeopardize my employment—all because of song lyrics in a talent show.

When You Need to Take a Stand

At the teacher's request, I listened to the lyrics of a talent show song that made fun of buying clothes from a thrift shop and was also filled with expletives in the "non-clean" version. Although even allowing clean versions was a problem for me (everyone knows where and when the swears arise in songs), the bigger issue was the song was neither kind nor inclusive for many of my students. Allowing two school values to be broken with the potential to make students wearing thrift clothes feel like outcasts simply was not an option for me.

This was far from a life-or-death problem, but it mattered. Knowing a group of parents would likely not accept my reasoning was not a compelling reason not to address the matter. And similar to the story of my Russian-speaking kindergartener who somehow didn't arrive at her bus stop, I needed to take all the responsibility for this failure for two reasons. First, I wanted to protect my staff members from their mistake. Second, ultimately, it *was* my mistake, because I was in charge everything that happened at our school, from arrival to dismissal.

I made the parent calls, leaning hard into our Fiske School value of inclusion as the foundation of my discussions. I explained I would not allow a song and dance with the potential to make students feel excluded. Some parents understood, others pushed back, saying we should have caught this mistake sooner, that it was unfair for students who had been practicing for more than a week to change an act, and I had to let them participate. I was steadfast in holding firm to our value of inclusion. The students' families decided collectively not to have their students participate and instead held a neighborhood talent show, which was fine with me. Although it was threatened, parents did not take the matter to the superintendent's office.

Only the affected students and their families knew what had happened, but I knew the courage necessary to uphold our value of inclusion was important in this instance. If I bowed to the pressure of a few parents' demands, I would not have been able to promote inclusion fully and authentically with my staff members and students. The headaches of multiple calls and even dealing with angry parents was worth it to me in the moment and in the days and weeks that followed.

The unpleasant, messy, and sometimes bureaucratic nonsense of education will reveal itself while you lead. It's what you do then that can matter most of all. Courage is answering "yes" when a teacher asks you to join in a parent-teacher conference because the parent makes her feel unsafe. Courage is refusing to take "no" for an answer from district leadership when you're trying to provide equity for students who need it. Courage is not blindly following a procedure that's on paper but doesn't consider important individual circumstances.

"Life Is What You Make of It"

The author Anaïs Nin said, "Life shrinks or expands in proportion to one's courage."[1] Kathy Baumgardner understands this, and she lives it with maximum courage. The reputation of Asbury Park High was that it was a scary, dangerous place, where no one—adults or children—wanted to be. As a new leader, she summoned her courage, knowing she had the power and responsibility to change lives and to do so with joy in her heart.

Although starting the school year with music and fun in hopes of changing a negative school culture doesn't neatly fit into a leadership skill set, it did mean something at Asbury Park High School. Simply put, it was a change from the new principal's perspective. Baumgardner wanted everyone to remember that school should be fun, even if it was hard. She wanted everyone to remember that these students were children, and not hardened criminals, as many of them had been treated by staff members in the past.

Given the license to create her own leadership team, Baumgardner had just one important question to ask them as she started her tenure: "What do you feel when you walk into this high school?" Answers varied, but they were overwhelmingly negative and included "a high level of fear," "anxiety," "sad," and "depression." These answers guided Baumgardner's vision to create a joyful school where learning happened and where order would be restored.

When she asked teachers the same questions about working at Asbury Park High School, their answers mirrored her team's responses. They blamed students and past administrators for allowing fear to pervade throughout the school. Baumgardner put the onus for change right back on her staff members. "In my world, life is what you make of it. You have the power to change the feeling and mood in your space. The building is my space and the classrooms are yours. Everyone who walks into this building needs to feel something besides anxiety, fear, and depression." Thus, what started with dancing into school became intentional plans to increase belongingness and shared mission, vision and values of teaching, learning, and leading.

Today and Tomorrow

Today. Find where your passions lie and what your values are. Then define and share these with your stakeholders. In doing so, you'll alert all to what you'll stand up for, plan for, and deliver on. In other words, you'll be setting the stage for what matters most for you and your followers. This can prompt you to act with courage when it's necessary to defend mission and values.

Tomorrow. Define, rewrite, or create system-wide values where you lead. In whatever form these values exist create further meaning by writing out discrete beliefs, mindsets, behaviors, or narratives that are an extension of your values. In doing so, you and your stakeholders will know the concrete actions, thoughts, and words that will require courage to identify, defend, and stick with through difficult circumstances.

Robert Bowman, the school leader who was highlighted in chapter 6, knew he had to make changes that required courage by disrupting the status quo of widespread failure at Harrison Middle School in Sunnyside, Washington. Bowman not only addressed a traditionally hot-button issue—grading—he enacted systemic changes that weren't punitive but thoughtful and compassionate. Having the courage to address student needs first, Bowman established a pathway for change when other important and ancillary matters arose as his middle school tried to improve student achievement.

Suggesting that F grades be dropped from teacher grading protocols was met with skepticism by many, just as removing other barriers such as participation, homework, and student behavior from grading had been a challenge earlier in his principalship. The arguments against removing F grades were typical—students received what they earned, taking away Fs is irresponsible, it's not fair for students who earn passing grades, and so on. In his heart and head, Bowman just knew F grades weren't helping students learn. In fact, the F was more than a grade; it was the branding and rein-forcement of considering oneself a failure.

Bowman fondly looks back on a change that took determination and convincing before greater student success was realized. "I could show you the incredible change in student culture once we removed Fs and failure from our grade books. When students saw their outcomes could improve through hard work and seeking help, I knew it was worth all the discussion and disagreement."

Refusing the Coward's Way Out

In chapter 1, we spent time with the Cleburne, Texas, ISD and saw how they spent time, effort, and energy developing their shared, system-wide values as a basis for all that they did—from finding students who didn't attend school during the early days of the 2020 pandemic to deeply diving into data that unearthed bias in discipline procedures. Having agreed-on values enabled the district to courageously address beliefs, mindsets, behaviors, and narratives that did not match their mission. In creating these values collectively and consistently referencing them, courage developed into an expected norm that became embedded in Cleburne's leadership team rather than just the thoughts or actions of individuals.

There is a challenge to holding all stakeholders to shared values because it raises accountability for all. If we hold each other accountable, then there is no room for anyone to fall short of those values at some point. Lack of skills to meet your values can also cause anxiety and disengagement. So just rolling out a bunch of new values won't make your department, school, or district better. You'll have to be courageous to confront stakeholders who don't live or model your values, as well as celebrate the instances when val-ues have made a difference in the life of a child or adult.

As Dr. Hickey, headmaster for Austin Prep in Reading, Massachusetts, described in chapter 7, it's important to state, restate, and find anecdotes that communicate mission and values, even if it engenders message fatigue in leaders. Just saying things in new ways can feel repetitive for leaders who can stray from effectively communicating to followers. One reason to stick with clearly communicating values is that when stakeholders disagree with a value, as happened to me in preparation for the school's talent show, you'll be ready with a quick and courageous response.

United Responses from Agreed-on Values

Dr. Hickey sees the leader's responsibility as being one of consistently walking disagreements back to agreed-on values. Even then, such attempts can blow up in a leader's face when discrepancies still remain unresolved. It's during those difficult moments when courage is most necessary, according to Dr. Hickey. "The mission and values are ours collectively, but leaders are the final judges for how those live in the school community. If we're not tightly aligned to values, we end up trying to be all things to all people."

There are so many cowardly ways out in education. A group of students score poorly on standardized tests, and we blame the children, their families, or entire social groups. Budgets need to be cut, and we ask building leaders or department heads to slash their supply costs, while adding further central office administration staff members to payroll. A superintendent reports to her entire administration team that only 44 percent of leaders trust more than one person in the room, eyes go to the floor, and the leader turns the page to the next agenda item.

The Impact of Cowardice

Worst of all, children who need us the most—those who feel marginalized or face discriminatory practices—can receive the least or be punished for who they are. Whether implicit or explicit, all social groups can suffer from the bias of adults in school and their greater communities. To believe they don't need more from us is to be ignorant to need and the ideals of this nation. Equity, as discussed previously, is not a nice "to-do activity" at the opening staff meeting; it's a roll-up-the-sleeves level of understanding and naming what's hindering children in school. Creating change to school culture and remedies that better suit all students' needs will require courage.

With equal parts courage and hope, Baumgardner took that initial step to change the climate and conditions at Asbury Park High School by having kids dance into school with teachers welcoming them. When Baumgardner looks back at her video from that day tears still well up in her eyes, because even though not everyone believed in her and what she was attempting to do, there were just enough seeds of change planted to keep her inspired.

After her 325 students danced into school, she had more in store for her seniors, who were greeted by breakfast in the media center. After they served themselves eggs, grits, waffles, and juice, Baumgardner announced her expectations for them all for the coming year—their opportunities for leadership, her belief in their achievement, and how the school would support them in their future plans.

For many staff members and students, it was a lot to take in. Some people voiced their displeasure by reiterating the high school wasn't a place for elementary school antics. But quietly during that first week, some teachers approached Baumgardner individually and would even whisper so as not be overheard, "Mrs. B., just want to say, I love what you're doing," and "That was really fun; I've never had a first day of school like that before."

Now Comes the Hard Part

It was about more than fun, of course. Baumgardner spent lots of time in the hallways, classrooms, and cafeteria to meet and get to know her students. She says the cafeteria was always a great spot to hang out, learn about the latest rap or pop sensation, or hear the gossip of the school. Just like Jim Walsh, my mentor from chapter 1, Baumgardner sprouted grassroots of change by better understanding who her students were and what they needed from her. She was also trying to live out the words adorning her office, "I hear you. I see you. You matter."

When students' tempers got the better of them, she offered to meet them during the school day to talk as an alternative to heated arguments with teachers. Because of this, it wasn't surprising for her to return from a district meeting off campus with a handful of students waiting to speak to her. They would usually start by demanding to know where she had been. Baumgardner would tell them, "You know I work here. This is my job," she said with smile.

Over time, mindfulness programming was brought into school to provide students with knowledge to recognize trauma-induced fight, flight, or freeze reactions and the tools to calm their minds through meditation and intentionally thinking about better ways to respond. It wasn't the curriculum, the data, or even the pedagogy that Asbury Park High School students needed first. It was simply Baumgardner's courage to start with student needs and then create plans from there.

But her courage didn't end there. Baumgardner also had some critical feedback for her staff members. Because she gave students the opportunity to leave class to seek her out, she found many of those students left or were sent to the principal's office after shouting matches with staff members. So, she put it on her teachers asking them, "What if I yelled at you in front of other staff members? You'd need medication or a shot of alcohol to calm yourself down." She instructed them to stop yelling and they did, but it took two years of reminders.

Speaking Her Mind

Another step in Baumgardner's leadership journey came at a staff meeting when the emotion of her words overtook her. At the time, Baumgardner was upset with the staff members' unwillingness to be flexible with their students. She wanted teachers to understand her anger and accept her call that they needed to be whatever students needed them to be—a nurse, mentor, mother, or father. Baumgardner had already modeled that she was willing to do anything to keep the building running—wiping tables in the cafeteria, covering classes when substitutes were short, or even mopping up vomit.

Now, at the faculty meeting she said, "Teaching is not for everybody. If you're not here for children in this building, then we don't need you to be here. I only want people here who want to do what's best for children. You have to be willing to be open and willing to be whatever your students need you to be in that moment."

As she expressed her frustration, Baumgardner felt a lump in her throat and felt tears in her eyes. "I got emotional and I started to cry, which I usually don't do." Although she wanted to express her passion, she did not plan on the emotion. It startled her, but she went with it.

The response was overwhelmingly positive. Some teachers apologized, and others thanked her for her passion, which they hadn't seen or felt from a leader in many years. Although she felt uncomfortable, Baumgardner knew she had to tap into her courage to carry on.

The results: Asbury Park High School's graduation rates continued to rise. Enrollment, which had been at an all-time low, rose considerably. Suspension rates declined by 200 percent. Suddenly, teachers throughout the district were clamoring to join Baumgardner's staff. And all of it started with her willingness to work through her fears and courageously curate a place of learning and belongingness for all.

The Seeds of Courage

All the leaders in this book had to answer a call to be courageous. Some found it in the means of communicating well and creating expectations; others in defining equity and belongingness or even in using the words "I love you." Every one of these leaders, from rural to urban neighborhoods, affluence to poverty, or successful to struggling systems, faced instances in which they had to consciously decide how to behave. Regardless of circumstance, they were unified in the need to be courageous at some point.

Your willingness to lead well is steeped in the seeds of courage. Anyone who has made the transition or is even considering moving into a leadership position has to understand how courage will work through you and show itself to your stakeholders. A willingness to stand for something means everything to those you lead.

I have taught and led with the intention of improving the lives of those I served. In these pages I have invoked the stories of my journey and the stories of those who have moved me in a meaningful way to be better, from five-year-olds to retired superintendents. It's my hope that this collective narrative, gathered from leaders from the four corners of our nation and everywhere in between, has inspired you to think, reflect, and create more informed ways of leading that make sense to you.

Embarking on this quest to codify and quantify what it means to lead fully through rational thoughts and heartfelt emotion—your head and heart—has pushed me to reconsider my story as I wrote it. I had to dig deeper into my memories and experience to consider if my leadership was effective, what made it so, as well as consider where did I go wrong and what did I learn from those experiences. And the process of writing and rewriting your own leadership based on experience, faith, research, and your own circle of influencers will carry on long after you've put this book down. At points reaffirm your path, pause to refocus when necessary, or commit yourself to learn something so breathtaking that it will disrupt your perspective, ensuring growth for all.

You carry the weight of responsibility, and it can be heavy. The load lightens with greater understanding of your place, your people, and most of all your students. Lead well. It's within you.

Reflections on How Life Should Be

- Like a muscle, courage needs to be exercised.
- Principal Kathy Baumgardner had to use courage to introduce the concept of joy into a skeptical, low-performing school—and she realized tremendous results.
- When you feel stuck, you can call on a mentor or expert for help, but in leadership you'll ultimately have to find the courage to do what's best.
- In my example of the exclusionary lyrics at the school talent show, I showed how sometimes the leader has to take responsibility for something a team member has done.
- Dr. Hickey, headmaster for Austin Prep, sees the leader's responsibility as being one of consistently walking disagreements back to agreed-on values.

Notes

Chapter 1

1. Dweck, C. S. (2007). *Mindset: The new psychology of success* (Updated ed.). Ballantine.

Chapter 2

1. Howard, T. C. (2010). *Why race and culture matter in schools.* Teachers College Press.
2. Stanford University Medical Center. (2007, March 5). Severe PTSD damages children's brains, study shows. *ScienceDaily.* www.sciencedaily.com /releases/2007/03/070304115131.htm
3. Bennett, C. (2007, Aug. 27). Effective praise in the classroom. ThoughtCo. thoughtco.com/effective-praise-8161
4. Chen, C. (2015, Oct. 27). Starting in Brookline, math program quickly adds up. *Boston Globe.* https://www.bostonglobe.com/metro/regionals /west/2015/10/02/starting-brookline-math-project-quickly-adds /lb3ZRISKfhdxuCfLWVo10I/story.html
5. Hattie ranking: 252 influences and effect sizes related to student achievement. Visible Learning. Retrieved August 25, 2020, from https://visible-learning .org/hattie-ranking-influences-effect-sizes-learning-achievement/

Chapter 3

1. Byrne-Jiménez, M., & Yoon, I. (2019, Jan. 9). Leadership as an act of love: Leading in dangerous times. *Frontiers in Education.* https://www .frontiersin.org/articles/10.3389/feduc.2018.00117/full
2. Baldwin, J. (1963). *The fire next time.* The Dial Press.
3. King, M. L. (2003). *A testament of hope: The essential writings and speeches* (Reprint ed.). Harper One.

Chapter 4

1. The right mindset for success. (2012, Jan. 12). *Harvard Business Review IdeaCast* (Episode 283 starting at 7:20). https://hbr.org/podcast/2012/01/the-right-mindset-for-success
2. National Center for Children in Poverty. (2018). United States demographics of low-income children. Retrieved December 17, 2020, from https://www.nccp.org/demographic/?state=US
3. Edmondson, A. C. (2004). *Psychological safety, trust, and learning in organizations: A group-level lens.* In R. M. Kramer & K. S. Cook (Eds.), *Trust and distrust in organizations: Dilemmas and approaches* (pp. 239–272). Russell Sage Foundation.

Chapter 6

1. Civil Rights Data Collection. (n.d.). 2015–16 state and national estimations, advanced placement. https://ocrdata.ed.gov/estimations/2015-2016. Although Latinx students make up 26 percent of the US student population, they are 21 percent of AP students. Black students are 15 percent of the population and make up 9 percent of AP students.
2. Roy, J. (2019). Engineering by the numbers. American Society for Engineering Education. https://ira.asee.org/wp-content/uploads/2019/07/2018-Engineering-by-Numbers-Engineering-Statistics-UPDATED-15-July-2019.pdf
3. CDC. (2016). *Sexual identify, sex of sexual contacts, and health-risk behaviors among students in grades 9–12: Youth risk surveillance.* US Department of Health and Human Services.
4. Civil Rights Data Collection. (n.d.). 2015–16 state and national estimations, discipline, out of school suspension. https://ocrdata.ed.gov/estimations/2015-2016. Black students, who are 15 percent of the national school population, make up 37 percent of out of school suspensions. Note: US Secretary to Education Betsy DeVos instructed the Office of Civil Rights to stop collecting discipline data.
5. Foster, L. (2019). Disproportionality and punishment: A CRE approach to school discipline. NYU Metropolitan Center for Research on Equity and the Transformation of Schools. https://steinhardt.nyu.edu/metrocenter/perspectives/disproportionality-and-punishment-cre-approach-school-discipline-2019#:~:text=Despite%20comprising%2067%20percent%20of,the%202017%2D18%20school%20year
6. Steele, C. M. (2011). *Whistling Vivaldi: How stereotypes affect us and what we can do* (Reprint ed.). W. W. Norton & Co.

7. Massachusetts Department of Elementary and Secondary Education. (n.d.). *Education tests for educator licensure (2018–2019)*. https://www.doe.mass.edu/mtel/annual/2019resultsbycategory.html

8. Frontline. (2012). *Middle school moment*. PBS. https://www.pbs.org/wgbh/frontline/article/middle-school-moment

Chapter 7

1. Didion, J. (1979). *The white album*. Simon & Schuster.

2. King, S. (2000). *On writing: A memoir of the craft*. Charles Scribner Sons.

Chapter 8

1. Nin, A. (2009). *The diary of Anais Nin* (Vol. 3: 1939–1944). Harcourt Brace Jovanovich.

Reflections